D1515853

'Buist and Lenning have made a major contribution to the criminological literature with *Queer Criminology*. It moves beyond the stereotypes that still characterize much criminological writing on the experiences of queer people in justice systems, reviewing the path-breaking theoretical and empirical contributions by the leaders in this emerging field. This will undoubtedly be the foundational text cited by every credible criminologist in years to come.'

Molly Dragiewicz, *Associate Professor, School of Justice, Faculty of Law, Queensland University of Technology, Australia*

'This first book on queer criminology couldn't be more relevant. Enough scholarship has been amassed to write such a book and the authors capably address queer people as victims, offenders, and criminal legal system workers. *Queer Criminology* is interdisciplinary and intersectional and also accessible to readers unfamiliar with the topic. This book should be required reading for every criminology scholar and criminal legal system worker.'

Joanne Belknap, *Professor of Ethnic Studies, University of Colorado-Boulder, USA*

'This volume is nothing short of groundbreaking. Not only do Buist and Lenning document how criminologists and the criminal legal system have historically ignored or marginalized LGBTQ communities and the experiences of LGBTQ victims and offenders, but they offer a clear and compelling framework for an inclusive criminology. There are no more excuses for the oversights and slights. The insights of *Queer Criminology* are certain to enrich criminological theory and serve as a springboard for significant, pioneering criminological research.'

Claire Renzetti, *Professor & Chair of Sociology, Endowed Chair in the Center for Research on Violence Against Women, University of Kentucky, USA*

QUEER CRIMINOLOGY

In this book, Carrie L. Buist and Emily Lenning reflect on the origins of Queer Criminology, survey the foundational research and scholarship in this emerging field, and offer suggestions for the future. Covering topics such as the criminalization of queerness, the policing of Queer communities, Queer experiences in the courtroom, and the correctional control of Queer people, *Queer Criminology* synthesizes the work of criminologists, journalists, legal scholars, nongovernmental organizations, and others to illuminate the historical and contemporary context of the Queer experience.

Queer Criminology offers examples of the grave injustices that Queer people face around the world, particularly in places such as Russia, Kyrgyzstan, England, India, Thailand, Nigeria, and the United States. These injustices include, but are not limited to, selective enforcement, coerced confessions, disproportionate sentencing, rape, extortion, denial of due process, forced isolation, corporal punishment, and death. By highlighting a pattern of discriminatory, disproportionate, and abusive treatment of Queer people by the criminal legal system, this book demonstrates the importance of developing a criminology that critiques the heteronormative systems that serve to oppress Queer people around the world.

Buist and Lenning argue that criminology is incomplete without a thorough recognition and understanding of these Queer experiences. Therefore, *Queer Criminology* is a vital contribution to the growing body of literature exploring the Queer experience, and should be considered a necessary tool for students, scholars, and practitioners alike who are seeking a more just criminal legal system.

Carrie L. Buist is an Assistant Professor of Criminology at the University of North Carolina Wilmington. Her research interests include Queer issues in criminology and criminal justice, media and crime, policing, feminism, and the sociology of pop culture. She has published in several peer-reviewed journals and served as co-editor for *Critical Criminology: An International Journal*'s special edition on Queer(ing) Criminology.

Emily Lenning is an Associate Professor of Criminal Justice at Fayetteville State University. Her publications cover a diverse range of topics, from state-sanctioned violence against women to creative advances in pedagogy. Her accomplishments in and out of the classroom have been recognized by several awards, including the North Carolina Criminal Justice Association's Margaret Lang Willis Outstanding Criminal Justice Educator Award and the American Society of Criminology Division on Women & Crime's New Scholar Award.

New Directions in Critical Criminology
Edited by Walter S. DeKeseredy, West Virginia University, USA

This series presents new, cutting-edge critical criminological empirical, theoretical, and policy work on a broad range of social problems, including drug policy, rural crime and social control, policing and the media, ecocide, intersectionality, and the gendered nature of crime. It aims to highlight the most up-to-date authoritative essays written by new and established scholars in the field. Rather than offering a survey of the literature, each book takes a strong position on topics of major concern to those interested in seeking new ways of thinking critically about crime.

QUEER
CRIMINOLOGY

Carrie L. Buist and Emily Lenning

Routledge
Taylor & Francis Group

LONDON AND NEW YORK

First published 2016
by Routledge
2 Park Square, Milton Park, Abingdon, Oxon, OX14 4RN

and by Routledge
711 Third Avenue, New York, NY 10017

Routledge is an imprint of the Taylor & Francis Group, an informa business

British Library Cataloguing-in-Publication Data
A catalogue record for this book is available from the British Library

Library of Congress Cataloging-in-Publication Data
Buist, Carrie L.
    Queer criminology / Carrie L. Buist and Emily Lenning.—First Edition.
      pages cm.—(New directions in critical criminology ; 13)
    1. Sexual minorities.   2. Criminology.   3. Criminal justice,
Administration of.   I. Lenning, Emily.   II. Title.
    HQ73.B85 2015
    306.76—dc23
    2015017526

ISBN: 978-1-138-82436-2 (hbk)
ISBN: 978-1-138-82437-9 (pbk)
ISBN: 978-1-315-74069-0 (ebk)

Typeset in Bembo
by Apex CoVantage, LLC

We dedicate this book to all of the Queer people who continue to confront and experience injustice around the globe. We applaud all those who have fought for and continue to fight for equality, and we challenge our students and colleagues to advocate for a more just criminal legal system.

CONTENTS

ACKNOWLEDGMENTS

We would first like to thank Walter DeKeseredy for believing in the importance of a queer criminology and the contributions that it has and will continue to make in the field of critical criminology. Next, we want to thank our team at Routledge. We would like to thank Thomas Sutton for his support and Heidi Lee for her constant guidance and dedication to the project. This book benefited from the thoughtful critique of reviewers and we appreciate the time they took to share with us their thoughts and suggestions. We are especially grateful to Sara Brightman, Chez Rumpf, and Bob Lenning for their feedback on earlier drafts of the manuscript, Cam Dyer for his tireless attempts to translate foreign documents, and to our graduate assistants, Regina Cline, Tyler McCarty, and Shanita Melvin for their research assistance. Thank you to Susan Caringella for her mentorship. This book would not have been possible without the support of our colleagues at the University of North Carolina Wilmington and Fayetteville State University. We acknowledge Jordan Blair Woods, Matthew Ball, Angela Dwyer, Vanessa Panfil, Chriss Galvin-White, and all of the scholars, practitioners, and students who are working and living queer criminology every day, with special recognition to Aimee Wodda, whose random conversation with me (Carrie) about queer criminology was instrumental in this process. We would also like to thank Human Rights Watch for their permission to reproduce previously published material in this book. Finally, we wish to recognize the members of the Division on Women and Crime of the American Society of Criminology whom we consider mentors, colleagues, friends, and a constant source of inspiration and encouragement. And finally, big up to Amanda Burgess-Proctor, Molly Dragiewicz, and Joanne Belknap who inspire us and who we can always count on for a good laugh at every ASC.

Carrie

First I would like to thank Emily Lenning, whose dedication and friendship knows no bounds. I would also like to extend my sincere thanks to Paul Leighton, Marilyn Corsianos, Jennifer Hatten-Flisher, Angie Moe, Susan Carlson, and Ron Kramer who have all served as invaluable mentors and inspirations to me personally and professionally, and who I consider myself lucky to call my dear friends. I would also like to express my appreciation to Adrienne Trier-Bieniek, Codie Stone, and thank my supportive colleagues at UNCW, especially the women's Thursday function. My deepest gratitude is extended to my family of friends who love me unconditionally and support me even though they have little to no idea what I am doing half of the time: To my road trip companions, Jackie Doyon and Liz Bradshaw who are crazy enough to drive across the country with me. To Mariliee Calhoun, Heather Robinson and all of the Beaver Creek girls past, present, and future. Thank you to my "LYBF" Sarah Scott who is the best person I've ever known. To Jeff Scott, Charley Scott, and the entire Proctor family. To my "grace" Jessica Edel who will forever be the rooster, and to the Gun Lake crew. Finally, I would like to thank my family: RN, thank you for taking me to my first Ramones concert. And, saving the best for last: I would especially like to thank my Mom, Sherry Buist, and my Gram, Mary Buist, for being shining examples of what strong, courageous, and hysterically funny women look like.

Emily

First and foremost, I would like to recognize and thank my wife. Shay, you are my greatest inspiration and source of support, and I am a better person because of you. Next, I must acknowledge that I would not be where I am today if not for the constant encouragement of my family, especially my parents, Nancy and Pete Grendze, Bob Lenning, and Jim McClatchy. Thank you for always telling me that there was nothing I couldn't do, for pushing me to reach for the stars, and for teaching me to be proud of who I am. To my BFF Sara Brightman, I owe you a debt of gratitude. Thank you for bringing me joy when I am sad, for celebrating every accomplishment (no matter how small), for being a strong woman that I can look up to and strive to be like, and for blessing me with the type of friendship that most people spend their entire lives searching for. So many friends have supported me throughout this project and to those who are not named here – please know that your assistance and support does not go unnoticed. To my Fayetteville State family – especially Beth Quinn, Miriam Delone, Michael DeValve, Chris Donner, Bonnie Grohe, Joe Brown, Beth Bir, Brandi Berry, Marquita Smith, Sandra Woodard, Karen McElrath, David & Lisa Barlow, and Jon Young – thank you for being amazing colleagues and friends. Last, but certainly not least, thank you to Carrie Buist for your friendship, for taking on this daunting project, for always putting up with me, and for believing in not just me, but in us.

GLOSSARY*

Bisexual: A person who is sexually, emotionally, and relationally attracted to more than one sex and/or gender.

Cisgender: An individual whose gender identity is consistent with their biological sex.

Compulsory Heterosexuality: The idea that heterosexuality is mandated and reinforced by our social institutions.

Gay: A man who is sexually, emotionally, and relationally attracted to other men. It is also an umbrella term used to denote members of the lesbian, gay, and bisexual community.

Heteronormativity: Formal and informal systems of cultural bias that favor heterosexuality.

Homophobia/Transphobia: An irrational fear or prejudice against members of the Queer community.

Intersex: Individuals born with ambiguous genitalia or sexual anatomy that does not fit the typical definition of male or female.

Lesbian: A person who is sexually, emotionally, and relationally attracted to other women.

LGBTQI: Lesbian, Gay, Bisexual, Transgender, Queer or Questioning, Intersex.

Patriarchy: A social system characterized by inequality in which men dominate formal institutions.

Transgender: An umbrella term used to describe individuals whose gender identities, expressions, and presentations differ from their biological sex.

Queer: An umbrella term used to describe anyone whose behavior or expression challenges notions of binary gender and/or heteronormative constructs.

Note

★ *These definitions do not represent the myriad of sexual and/or gender identities that are possible and the numerous individualized ways in which people choose to identify and/or express sexuality and/or gender.*

1

QUEER(ING) CRIMINOLOGY

Queer criminology is a theoretical and practical approach that seeks to highlight and draw attention to the stigmatization, the criminalization, and in many ways the rejection of the Queer community, which is to say the LGBTQ (lesbians, gay, bisexual, transgender, and queer) population, as both victims and offenders, by academe and the criminal legal system (see Ball 2014a; Buist & Stone 2014; Groombridge 1998; Peterson & Panfil 2014b, Tomsen 1997; Woods 2014). Although there is no question that persons who identify as part of the Queer community have been included in research samples, "their sexual and/or gender identities are not interrogate[d] as salient characteristics, as these are likely not recognized at all" (Peterson & Panfil 2014b: 3). Thus, queer criminology seeks to both move LGBTQ people, to borrow from bell hooks, from the margins to the center of criminological inquiry, and to investigate and challenge the ways that the criminal legal system has been used as a tool of oppression against Queer people.

Criminological research and the criminal legal system have ignored the experiences of Queer people in any real, substantive way: Except for the focus on sexual proclivities as deviant – a presumption that was posited by early criminologists, such as Cesare Lombroso in the 1800s, and subsequently influenced much of criminological and sociological research on gay, lesbian, bisexual, transgender, and queer people (Woods 2014). Further, Jordan Blair Woods has posited in the formation of his homosexual deviancy theory that the ways in which Queer people were treated within early criminological theory influenced how "baseless stereotypes and social biases shaped definitions of 'criminal behavior' and 'criminal populations'" (Woods 2015: 133). Woods's theory consists of two major components, the first component, *the deviance-centered element*, notes that, until the 1970s, any focus within criminological theory and research that was given to Queer populations was couched within the assumption that Queer people were deviant. He goes on to remind us that, during this time, there were "dominate external legal, political, and societal mechanisms of social control that defined Queer populations as deviants in different ways . . . criminal anti-sodomy laws, medical conceptions of homosexuality as mental illness, and sociological conceptions of homosexuality as products of failed socialization patterns" (Woods 2015: 133).

The second component of Woods's (2015) theory contains the *invisibility element*, which posits that research on Queer people and on sexual orientation and gender identity essentially disappears from the landscape, particularly after the 1970s. According to Woods (2015: 135), this invisibility led to "changing attitudes about sexual deviance" but, regardless of the disappearance or the change in focus about sexual deviance, Woods reminds us that, historically, sexual orientation and/or gender identity have been researched and theorized within a deviancy framework, and, regardless of the changes that have taken place, these historical and cultural presumptions about Queer people and the Queer community continue to influence the ways in which Queer folks are treated in the field.

Woods's theory draws attention to the historical roots of homophobia within criminology as a discipline, while also bringing to light the present concerns within the field based on the lack of research conducted on Queer people and their experiences within the criminal legal system and within criminology in general. This *invisibility* breeds complacency within the field and allows us to further ignore the experiences of Queer people. In this book, we offer examples of the plethora of experiences that Queer folks have within the criminal legal system in an effort to bring this population from the margins to the center of focus.

While we offer you a definition of queer criminology, it would be remiss of us to assume that this is the *only* definition. At the time of this writing, queer criminology is a developing subdiscipline within criminology broadly and, as many believe, critical criminology more specifically. In fact, *all* of what might characterize the field has not yet come to fruition. Generally speaking, one might say this book is a reflection of where the field is. It is a beginning – reflections on a variety of queer-focused issues in criminological research and theory meant to spark and advance an important conversation. So, while some have demanded that queer criminology have a narrow, rigid definition – we could not disagree more. We believe that the definition of queer criminology should be broad and dynamic and remain so in order to reflect the fluidity of the Queer identity and therefore allow for a variety of contributions both theoretically and via practical application in the field.

Until then, it is important to address the use of *Q(q)ueer*, which you will note we use throughout this book as an umbrella term to capture lesbians, gays, bisexuals, transgender folks, intersex folks, and any others who fall outside of the heteronormative gender binary. We recognize that not everyone who identifies as lesbian, gay, bisexual, or transgender also identify as Queer. We further recognize that the reasons why some individuals may or may not identify with or simply agree with the use of Queer vary, and that for some, those reasons are deep-seated at the cultural level – often experiencing rejection (although not entirely) by communities of color. In this sense, even language that is meant to be inclusive has the potential to divide, which brings up perhaps the most problematic aspect of queer criminology: Language. The word *queer* makes some people cringe but others prefer the use of the word as a means of deconstruction and inclusivity. Others still may furrow their brows by the complexity of it all. We want to make clear that we do not use this word to offend or bother – we do this understanding the power of language and how it can be either inclusive or exclusionary. We use it with the intention of the former rather than the latter, and even though we, as mentioned, understand that some may disagree, we want to remind you that the use of the word *queer* and its general definition have evolved over time. It should be noted that where we have used an acronym (e.g. LGBT) in lieu of queer, it is because the authors and research-ers we are citing have used that acronym and we want to accurately reflect their population of focus and respect that they likely have legitimate reasons for focusing on specific identities.

We also offer the word to you for consideration as something that differs from the norm and we would suggest that queer criminology is and can be theory, research, or praxis that falls outside the norms of criminological research. As mentioned, while criminologists have been theorizing about and researching the experiences of the queer community for much of the last century (although the amount of research is still scant and the focus of the research is myopic), it is not "out of the norm" to do so. What is historically out of the norm is to do so from a position of critique – for example, recognizing and highlighting the *construction* of Queer identities as deviant and crimi-nal, questioning the state's role in criminalizing sexual orientation and/or gender identity, or exploring the role of the criminal legal sys-tem as a mechanism for the social control of Queer identities. A truly queer criminology moves beyond the traditional deviance framework and shifts the spotlight from the rule breakers to the rule makers (see Ball 2014b; Woods 2014).

Language and identity

First and foremost, we must point out that sex and gender are two different things. As indicated by Lenning (2009), sex describes the DNA and sex organs that we are born with, while gender is distin-guished by our actions and thus should be recognized as a verb. In other words, gender is a social construction characterized by outward presentation of masculinity, femininity, or anything in between. Sex is a biological fact determined by genetic codes and physical anatomy. Further, neither gender nor sex are inextricably linked to one's sexual orientation, meaning that your sex or gender does not determine who you are emotionally, relationally, and sexually attracted to.

At this point in history, one can find literally hundreds of words used to describe various sexual and gender identities, and the list continues to grow. Though most commonly used to represent the Queer community, the "LGBT" acronym is simply not representative of all members of the Queer community. As Lenning (2009) found in her study that included 249 transidentified individuals, participants used no less than 23 terms to describe their own gender identity. Even their romantic partners, most of whom were presumably cis-gender, used a dozen terms to describe their own gender identity. When asked to identify their sexual orientation, the answers were just as varied. What Lenning (2009) concluded, at least in regards to gender identity, is that, at the very least, researchers need to identify an individual's gender orientation *and* gender presentation in order to even begin to understand trans experiences. She notes that "Because our gender is a combination of both our gender orientation and our gender presentation, which are sometimes at odds with one another, sociological research needs to begin considering these dimensions as separate, yet equally important, aspects of our research participant's identities" (Lenning 2009: 52). Even still, to do so is only to scratch the surface of understanding how dimensions of our gender, let alone our sexuality, affect one's experiences with and within the criminal legal system.

We must keep in mind that, for some, sexual orientation is not a fixed label or identity, and, therefore, we use what is meant to be more inclusive language in an attempt to promote understanding at both the interpersonal and structural levels. In the most general sense, we reject essentialist attitudes because they fail to fully recognize sexual and gender identity and its fluidity among some Queer individuals, especially trans folk. For example, if someone who was born female and identifies as a lesbian transitions to male yet still chooses romantic relationships with women, is that person still identified as a lesbian or is that person identified as heterosexual? Certainly, the only person who can accurately answer that question would be the person who has experienced this transition. While fairly uncomplicated, this example speaks to the importance of identifying the influence of queer theory on queer criminology – certainly we contend that, if nothing else, some of the central tenets of the theory should be considered when addressing the whys of queer criminology. As noted by Jagose (1996: 3) "queer theory's debunking of stable sexes, genders, and sexualities develops out of a specifically lesbian and gay rework-ing of the post structuralist figuring of identity as a constellation of multiple and unstable positions." Therefore, returning to the example given, while sexual orientation and gender identity may be easily identifiable and definable for some, they are not for others. Further, how an outsider looking in may define or identify another may be wholly inaccurate; therefore, it is important to understand the complexities of categorization. For instance, it is always problematic when we make assumptions regarding one's sexual orientation or gender identity.

There are, of course, the biological arguments and considerations regarding sexual orientation – which posit that an individual does not choose who they are sexually, emotionally, and relationally attracted to. Conversely, there are the socialization-centered arguments that one's sexual orientation and/or gender identity are constructed within the formal and informal, cultural, institutional, and structural elements within society that influence one's personal decisions regarding who they choose to be sexually, emotionally, and relationally attracted to. There are indeed pros and cons to each of these arguments, and, quite frankly, instead of making broad and sweeping generalizations about sexual orientation and/or gender identity, we contend that it does not really matter. What matters is that we do have a significant percentage of the world's population who identify as gay, lesbian, bisexual, transgender, and queer, and as individuals and taken together, that community has experienced and continues to experience differential and disproportionately negative experiences within the criminal legal system from all aspects of the system – as offenders, victims, agents, and within academe.

Further, in general, there is no debate over whether or not heterosexual people are born that way or have chosen that identity because we live in a world where heterosexuality is normative and compulsory. We ask those of you who continue to debate the sexual orientation and/or gender identities of others to look inward and think about your own. But more so, we challenge you to understand that, regardless of these debates, what is known, what is a social fact that we are addressing here, is that Queer people continue to have fewer human rights and liberties than heterosexual and gender-conforming people, and that, based solely on sexual orientation and/or gender identity, people continue to face discrimination, harassment, victimization, torture, and even death in the United States and abroad. If for no other reason, this is why there needs to be a queer criminology.

Within a developing field of study, the ongoing debate regarding how a queer criminology should look can be problematic and this will be revisited below after we discuss some of the potential criminological allies within the field today.

Feminist and critical criminology

First, feminist criminology is a critical criminology, but even upon the development of radical and critical criminology in the 1960s, women's issues were still on the periphery of knowledge. Therefore, we seek to identify some of the specific ways in which feminist criminology, which has developed into a widely used and respected approach to criminological inquiry, and queer criminology are similar. At the core of feminist criminology is a belief that gender is and should be a primary concern of criminological research. Early feminist criminology leaned towards the liberal feminist ideals of inclusion in mainstream criminological research and development of feminist theoretical approaches that included the hotly debated emancipation/liberation theories of Adler (1975) and Simon (1975). These theories posited that greater equality and independence for women would lead to their increased criminality. However, these theories, among others, were problematic – much like the liberal feminist agenda within the women's movement. Other theories that explored the influence of family structure on girls and boys, such as Hagan, Simpson, and Gillis's (1987) study, examined power-control theory in the household, which also explored class structure as well. Feminist criminology argued, rightly so, that girls and women were ignored in the existing research but the assumption at the time was that theories that were developed from research conducted on males could yield the same findings for women. This "add women and stir" (Chesney-Lind 1988) approach, as we came to learn, would simply not suffice. Neither will "add Queer and stir" (Ball 2014a) approaches sufficiently explain Queer experiences in the criminal legal system. Different feminist approaches to research would have to be used if we wanted to uncover and highlight the unique experiences of girls and women and the many factors and variables involved in their experiences that could contribute to the offending, the victimization, or the unique experiences as women working in male-dominated fields. Therefore, as we began to see more critical approaches to feminist criminology develop, such as utilizing socialist feminist theory to highlight the problematics associated with capitalism and patriarchy, or Black feminist theory to remind us of the importance of intersectionality, we saw more in-depth research produced. Similarly, we are likely to see queer criminology evolve into a broad range of theoretical and methodological perspectives as it becomes a more complete and established area of criminology.

For example, look at the substantial research that feminist criminologists have contributed to our understanding of the unique factors that impact girls and women differently than boys and men – the feminist pathways approach to research, for example, highlights several pathways that often influence and contribute to female offending such as race, class, history of abuse, drug use, mental illness, and so on. The impact of these factors play a unique role in their experiences within the criminal legal system and attention to the cycle of violence and the impact that victimization has on female offenders are key tenets of the approach (Belknap & Holsinger 1998; Belknap & Holsinger 2006; Brennan, Breitenbach, & Dieterich 2010; Daly 1992; Mallicoat 2015). Queer folks also experience unique pathways to offending that in many ways relate specifically to their sexual orientation and/or gender identity. For example, as the forthcoming chapters will show, as young Queer boys and girls come out to their families, they are often kicked out of their homes by disapproving family members. Queer youth also experience disproportionate levels of bullying in school that can lead to suspension or expulsion. Further, they are more likely to attempt suicide than their heterosexual peers. These experiences can lead to arrest and/or criminal labels and further stigmatization unique to Queer young people.

Again, we understand and agree that feminist criminology is a critical criminology, and as we have highlighted the important overlap between the inception of feminist criminology and the need for queer criminology, it is important to recognize the failures within critical criminology to include women at the onset of the development of the discipline, just as Queer folks have essentially been left out as well. We ask, why hasn't critical criminology been researching or theorizing or, at the very least, discussing this topic for the last 30-plus years? Why is it that this concept of a queer criminology has just recently (within less than ten years) reached the critical criminological landscape? Certainly, seminal articles on the topic were first published in the late 1990s (Groombridge 1998; Tomsen 1997), but the first time we saw any real attention from critical criminology on the topic was just recently in 2014 when the journal *Critical Criminology* dedicated a special edition to Queer/ing Criminology. Further, while at the time of this writing we have seen other publications that focus on LGBT experiences within the criminal legal system, namely Mogul, Ritchie, and Whitlock's (2011) *Queer (In)Justice: The Criminalization of LGBT People in the United States* and Peterson and Panfil's (2014a) edited monolithic *Handbook of LGBT Communities, Crime, and Justice* and we are certain to see more soon, the research on this population has been limited and the reception from colleagues has been lukewarm.

We are not implying that we (queer criminologists) have not been supported, as clearly there is some support or you would not be reading this today, but it is problematic that a critical criminology that was developed in reaction to the lack of attention paid towards the influence of class and power would be slow to support such an endeavor like queer criminology. Again, we are reminded that critical criminology, as we have come to know it today, developed from the radical criminological perspectives developed in the 1960s as a response to mainstream criminology's tendency to ignore the influence of the powerful (Buist & Stone 2014; Lynch & Michalowski 2000). Further, as noted by Leighton (2010: 16), "when you are the power you shape people's vision of the truth." These perspectives are integral to concepts within not only queer theory, which we will discuss in more detail below, but in the development of queer criminology as well. Questions often arise within the criminal legal system regarding who has the power and how those powerful people are the most politically influential. This in turn shapes policy and the implementation of policy that has for the most part worked to keep Queer people marginalized. Certainly, this is the case in over 78 countries around the world where same-sex consensual sex is illegal.

Influence of queer theory on queer criminology

Returning to the definition of queer criminology, we are aware, as previously mentioned, that while others may simply disagree with our definition, there are some who may be offended by the mere use of the term, *queer criminology*. While we are wholly concerned with highlighting and identifying the injustices that Queer people experience within the criminal legal system, and we are proponents of developing a queer criminology and supporting the myriad ways it looks, we are well aware of the prejudiced attitudes that are still alive in the United States and abroad regarding the Queer community. We also recognize, as noted, that for some people, the word *queer* invokes a visceral and negative feeling. For those who reject the term, we are left with the hope that people will approach this work with a critical lens and recognize the existence of compulsory heterosexuality and the influence of heteronormativity on the criminal legal system. That regardless of personal politics, an educated person will concede that given the historical and current climates at the global level, Queer people are faced with certain injustices both within and outside of the criminal legal system that heterosexual people do not experience because of their sexual orientation and/or gender identity. As mentioned, queer is something that has been considered outside of the norm, but it also represents the importance of fluidity and refusal to be labeled any one specific way. This approach relates to the influence that queer theory has had on the development of queer criminology.

Queer theory developed from a need to recognize that sexual identity mattered – on both the micro and macro levels of research, and that the lived experiences of an individual identifying as queer was a part of a larger social structure that categorized and labeled that identity. Instead of keeping queer at the periphery of knowledge and research, queer theory called for specific attention to be paid to "sexuality and gender as subjects worthy of consideration in their own right" (Kirsch 2000: n.p.). Certainly, queer theory wanted focus to be turned to sexuality and gender as topics of inquiry, but there was a deeper need for these explorations. One major influence of queer theory on queer criminology is that it is distinctive because, rather than simply introducing sexuality and gender orientation as a variable, queer criminological perspectives are/can be used as a lens through which to question the status quo. When we do this, we can begin to recognize that these identities have been used as structural mechanisms of social control. As noted by Rutter and Schwartz (2012: 27), "sexuality is never totally 'free' from its social context." Further, any discussion of labels, categories, or descriptives always have the possibility of influencing the ways in which we identify others, often times producing in and out groups, punishing others for behavior that is outside of the norm or, for purposes of queer theory and criminology, the hetero/binary norm (Ball 2014b; Rutter & Schwartz 2012).

As mentioned, we contend that queer criminology is also influenced by critical views in criminology. One of those topics includes, but is not limited to, power. Power with regard to sexuality is a topic that has been previously discussed in the literature. Indeed, Kirsch (2000) highlights the work of Foucault (among others) when discussing the importance of considering the influence of power on behavior. This is an important distinction to mention and it certainly supports our position that queer criminology is a critical criminology and should be thought of and respected as such. Radical criminologists predominately focused on class as the power differential that should be taken into account in criminological research. Sexual orientation and gender identity should also be viewed as identities that impact a power imbalance, especially when we are considering social capital. Topics such as equality and legal protections not only for victims, offenders, and practitioners within the criminal legal system but also regarding marriage, health care, employment, legal representation, harassment and so on, speak to the inequities within the United States and abroad. When the law allows for heterosexuals and cisgender individuals to have protections, rights, and opportunities that are not equally afforded to nonheteronormative individuals, the imbalance and the lack of agency and capital for the Queer community is undeniable.

As noted by Foucault (1980) and reiterated by Kirsch (2000), the oppressive nature of power inhibits the freedom of others. Recognition of this oppression certainly contributed to events such as the Stonewall Riots that took place on June 29, 1969. We will discuss this event later; briefly, the riots took place as police officers raided a local gay bar and, instead of peacefully disbanding, the gay and trans-gender patrons of the Stonewall Inn fought back against the police, and, subsequently, this event became the symbol for the gay libera-tion movement (Jagose 1996). Although this one event is heralded as the defining moment within the movement and the reason why gay pride is celebrated every June, we must not let this single event overshadow the cumulative efforts for equality and freedom during that time and thereafter.

For instance, during the 1960s and 1970s, there were two gay lib-eration movements that were beginning to take shape and influenced the cause. Jagose (1996: 30) details the differences in the two major movements within the gay community – first beginning in the 1960s in what was referred to as homophile organizations, which sought to slowly gain acceptance within heteronormative society, the main goals of the organizations were to eventually gain "legal and social recognition on the same terms as heterosexuals." While the riots at Stonewall Inn became known as the genesis of the gay liberation movement, the event was more of a coincidence rather than what spawned the movement. In contrast to the homophile movement, the gay liberation movement of the 1970s and 1980s was focused on achieving equality not through passivity and patience, but through demands and urgency. Here we see some similarity with the feminist movement both on the larger scale and within criminology as well. They began, as noted above, with the more liberal feminist approach that focused on equality and recognition within society and the disci-pline, and then moved to the more critical approaches such as socialist, radical, lesbian, and Black feminist theoretical approaches that focused on several different factors and variables related to inequality beyond legislation, such as capitalism, patriarchy, heterosexism, and race.

In many ways, this is where we stand today with regard to Queer rights and, in turn, this is where we stand with queer criminology. We assure you that as we are writing this book, we are the minority. At conferences, we are looked upon quizzingly when we discuss this field of research. Professionals in the field question if this is even a required area of research, teaching, or study. We are puzzled by this confusion but not surprised. That is why we make this call for a queer-focused criminology, because, as previously argued, the inequities within the United States and around the world between the heteronormative/

cisgender population and the Queer population are not only experienced through loss of social capital, but it is also experienced through the ways in which society, especially the criminal legal system, act in an effort to control the Queer population.

Even still, while queer theory was couched within the deconstruction of categories as Sedgwick (1990) contends, the binary categories that are used to describe the homo and hetero identities are often problematic, and people often do not exist within those binaries. Further, when we have these categorical distinctions grouped in those binaries, often times one of those categories are viewed as lesser than the other (Sedgwick 1990). We recognize the importance of deconstructing categories and worry, as Ball (2014a: 532) points out, that queer criminology does not specifically focus on deconstruction, which can be limiting in addressing injustice. Conversely, however, for some, categories can be empowering. They can bring people and groups together who experience similar inequalities and obstacles and breed new social movements. Certainly, deconstruction does matter, as even the language we use here may be problematic and deconstructing categories allows for a more organic way of knowing. However, as symbolic interactionism has taught us, we continue to construct meaning in our everyday lives in a variety of ways. Recall, as Green (2007) points out, that symbolic interactionists such as West and Zimmerman (1987) were "doing gender." And although Butler (1990) may be more identified as a queer theorist in her own right, her discussion of performativity is closely related to "doing gender" as we have now come to know it, but nevertheless examines the importance of discourse in understanding gender performance. This lends itself to the importance of language, as Sedgwick (1990: 17) indicates:

> . . . terminological complication is closely responsive to real ambiguities and struggles of gay/lesbian politics and identities: e.g., there are women-loving-women who think of themselves as lesbians but not as gay, and others who think of themselves as gay women but not as lesbians . . .

In brief, we tend to agree with Woods's (2014) assertion that queer criminology should be both "identity-driven" and deconstructionist. While, as Woods points out, this may be a problematic position to take, we agree that it allows for a wider range of research and theorizing to take place. As he notes, because sexual orientation and gender identity can be central to so many people's lives, focusing on these can assist in understanding the Queer experience and how there are unique experiences that this population faces. Conversely, focusing on deconstruction can allow for a better understanding of how concepts of sexual orientation and gender identity can combat assumptions of how these concepts are applied in criminological inquiry. We believe that Woods's approach is one that seeks inclusivity within the research while understanding the problems that may arise. Woods contends that it is important to provide thoughtful and critical insight into this field of research in order to avoid further stigmatization (see Woods 2014).

Thus, while we recognize the possibility of examining whether there is a need to "forge connections between queer theory and criminology" (Ball 2014a: 533) we are not completely convinced that this is a make-it or break-it requirement within the field of research, and would rather cast a wider net, again, with inclusivity in mind. However, with that being said, Ball (2014a: 533) further notes that queer theory is a field with both academic and political underpinnings that has "focused on charting the various forms of regulation through which we are shaped as subjects, particularly with regard to sexuality and gender . . . excavates the forms of (usually hetero) normativity that are embedded in social institutions and relations, and, drawing from post-structural thought, challenges essentialized notions of identity and identity politics. . . ." While gender and sexuality may be fluid for some, for others, it is absolutely fixed – therefore, while queer theory is influential in developing theoretical approaches to understanding and perhaps ultimately breaking down assumptive categories, we contend that it cannot be applied to queer criminology as a whole, because, quite simply, there are different ways to doing queer criminology just like there are different ways of doing critical criminology. For example, one might focus on the role of the state with regard to illegal dumping (Doyon 2014) or nuclear weapons (Kramer & Bradshaw 2011) or forced sterilization (Brightman, Lenning, & McElrath 2015) and although these topics differ, it does not make the research any less critical.

Deconstruction is also problematic because, quite frankly, we are probably never going to be in a world without categorical descriptions that are used in some way or another to provide an understanding of who people are. Is this beneficial? In some ways, of course not, in other ways, they are indeed beneficial. In a perfect world, we would not use categories, especially binary categories, but this world is far from perfect, and while one description, one label, one identity does not a person make, even without categories, we contend that there will always be meaning. We will continue to understand the world in which we live by constructing meaning and then giving significance to the people, the identities, the relationships, the knowledge, and so on, that we have come to know. Ferrell (2013: 258–259) contends that we assign meaning to the

> . . . contested social and cultural processes by which situations are defined, individuals and groups are categorized, and human consequences are understood . . . made in many ways – but following the insights of symbolic interactionists, we know that one of the primary ways is through social interaction in the situations of everyday life.

We give meaning to our everyday worlds within every milieu as Ferrell (2013) points out, from casual interactions to criminality and deviant behavior. Therefore, while we are well aware that this will continue to be debated, we contend that while Queer may mean one thing to someone, it means something quite different to another. However, when taking everything into account, perhaps those categorical descriptions can allow for marginalized groups to understand their marginalization in new ways and draw support from each other, moving them to the center of knowledge construction. When considering the deconstruction of categories, we come to understand that truth can be subjective, and, as pointed out earlier, truth can be molded to fit the needs of the powerful. It is our hope that by presenting the information we bring forth in this book, there is a collective understanding of the inequality that Queer folks face within the United States and abroad, particularly with and within the criminal legal system.

A glance at what's to come

In the chapters to come, we seek to highlight the experiences of Queer people as victims, offenders, and as practitioners. We do so using several different approaches to elucidating these experiences across the globe. Each chapter highlights the experiences of Queer folks as related to the criminal legal system throughout the world, attempting to draw attention to these problems and to make suggestions for changes that may improve the criminal legal system, but to also illuminate the changes that must be made at the structural and institutional levels in order to implement these changes. Legislation continues to be passed that criminalizes or, at the very least, marginalizes Queer people based solely on their sexual orientation and/or gender identity. Once we accept and realize that these discriminatory practices are done most often on large-scale institutional levels, our hope is that there will be a more clear understanding for the need to not only understand the Queer experience in a practical sense but at the theoretical level as well. Finally, in recognizing these injustices, the need for a queer criminology comes to light (See Ball 2014b; Woods 2014).

Beginning with Chapter 2, *Criminalizing queerness*, we examine the historical significance of sexual orientation and gender identity as related to the ways in which legislation has and continues to work to criminalize and therefore label and stigmatize Queer people, quite literally how "queerness" has been criminalized. For instance, it was not until the 2003 Supreme Court case, *Lawrence v. Texas*, that sodomy laws criminalizing homosexual sex were deemed unconstitutional in the United States. What's more, there are nearly 80 countries around the globe that currently have laws prohibiting consensual sex between members of the same sex, and some of those countries impose the penalty of death for such behavior. What we contend is that these laws represent a global culture of homophobia that continues to persist regardless of common sense opinions on how progressive current and future generations are and have become. What we mean by this is that as professors and researchers, we are well aware of the shifting opinions of many young people, especially in places like the United States, Canada, and the United Kingdom, regarding members of the Queer community and the rights that they should have. Further, because of this, it is often far too easy to assume that because opinion polls have indicated that most Americans support gay marriage that means that there is little to no concern over gay equal rights. This is as problematic as the assumption that racism in the United States has been eradicated because it has elected its first Black president. While improved public opinion is certainly an important step in the right direction, we cannot be complacent to the injustices and terrors that Queer people face around the world every single day based solely on their sexual orientation and/or gender identity.

This chapter will identify the deep-seated homophobia that historically reflected colonial British values and continues to influence anti-gay sentiment and legislation throughout the world, such as in Africa where nearly 40 countries have criminalized homosexuality. We will offer examples of bribery, police brutality, humiliation, threats, and extreme violence in a variety of countries, including Uganda, Kenya, Nigeria, and Russia – all of which are the result of, or committed in the name of, compulsory heterosexuality.

In addition to the criminalization of sexuality, Chapter 2 highlights how gender nonconformity has been criminalized around the globe. Historically and presently, these laws focus on individuals who are seen as "impersonating" the opposite sex. Obviously, these regulations have significant impact on the transgender population, and, therefore, trans men and women suffer the most from the enforcement of these laws. To explore the criminalization of gender nonconformity, this chapter will highlight important court cases where these laws have differentially impacted members of the Queer community who have been targeted for "imitating" the opposite sex or for "deception," and will highlight how Queer people are frequently blamed for their victimization based on their gender expression.

Chapter 3, *Queer criminology and law enforcement*, turns our focus to how law enforcement fails in protecting and serving members of the adult and juvenile Queer population. Research used will pay close attention to the lack of trust that Queer folks have of the police and the reasons why they feel suspicious and fearful of law enforcement officers and officials. We begin the chapter by calling attention to the tumultuous relationship between minority men and women and police officers and connote both the level of distrust that police officers have towards citizens and the level of distrust that citizens, more specifically marginalized populations, have towards law enforcement officials. Most recently, we have seen several newsworthy incidents involving police brutality towards young Black men in notable cases involving the deaths of Michael Brown in Ferguson, Missouri, and Eric Garner in New York City. While the police officers involved in these cases were not indicted for excessive force, the media has brought attention to the racism that likely incited these incidents. In a recent turn of events, in a March 2015 report on the investigation of the Ferguson Police Department, the Department of Justice (DOJ 2015: 2) found that the Ferguson police department had a history of aggressive policing tactics and noted in the report that police officials did not work within the law and infrequently addressed citizen complaints of officer wrong-doing. The DOJ (2015: 4) also found that the ways in which Ferguson's police department "reflects and reinforces racial bias including stereotyping." It further noted that the injurious behavior of the Ferguson police department and their "court practices are borne disproportionately by African Americans, and there is evidence that this is due in part to intentional discrimination on the basis of race" (2015: 4).

We feel it is important to address these issues regarding race because they highlight the ongoing and systemic prejudicial opinions and discriminatory practices that are pervasive within the criminal legal system. So, while we highlight these racist policing practices and note the influence of media campaigns such as #blacklivesmatter, we also bring to your attention the hashtag movement #blacktranslivesmatter. Although the latter is certainly far less known than the former, it is no less important. Transgender men and women, but especially trans women of color, experience physical and emotional abuse from police throughout the United States and abroad based solely on their gender identity. While society knows much about the brutal deaths of young men like Brown, Garner, and Tamir Rice, we still know little about how race, class, sexual orientation and gender identity intersect and impact the Queer community with regards to experiences with law enforcement.

Additionally, law enforcement officials who identify as LGBTQ have themselves experienced prejudice and discrimination on the job, although there is no evidence that indicates sexual orientation or gender identity has a negative impact on the ways in which officers perform their duties. Chapter 3 will discuss law enforcement from several different angles, first beginning with Queer civilian experiences with officers and officials, including police misconduct and brutality, followed by a discussion on the selective enforcement of Queer folks (both adults and juveniles). We highlight how police disproportionately target the gay population, which in turn increases the level of distrust between officers and Queer people. As mentioned, we will detail the unique experiences of LGBTQ law enforcement agents and explore changes in departmental policy that may benefit officers and ultimately the Queer people they are supposed to protect and serve.

Finally, we will discuss these problems as they relate to the hypermasculine policing subculture that values machismo over compassion and has historically failed to implement community policing in any real, effective way that truly incorporates and encapsulates civilian concerns and partnerships between officers and citizens. This chapter argues that if community policing were ever implemented correctly, it could introduce real change in the lives of the community members, gay and straight alike, and the officers as well. We will explore the different styles of policing and the culture of law enforcement and how this works to keep Queer folks on the margins while on the job. In addition to these complexities, we will explore locations abroad that have worked successfully towards bridging the gap between Queer folks and officers and policy implementation that has worked in creating acceptance and understanding of Queer officers in their departments.

Moving forward, Chapter 4 follows the progression within the criminal legal system from policing to courts. In *Queer criminology and legal systems*, we examine the myriad of ways in which the system has failed Queer folks regarding representation and equal protection under the law. As Chapter 2 explored the criminalization of queerness, this chapter will highlight how that criminalization and ultimately the denial of human rights, which significantly impacts agency and capital, are determined by overzealous prosecutors, inept defense attorneys, and biased judges. Legislation, which is ultimately decided upon in the court, can affect several different arenas in one's life, one such arena is that of employment. States without nondiscrimination clauses create an environment where Queer people have no recompense and can lose their jobs just because of their sexual orientation or gender identity. There has also been considerable backlash experienced by Queer people who lobby for gay marriage or who have been married, like the physical abuse experienced by a Michigan woman who was beaten after having appeared on the news regarding the state's ban on same-sex marriage.

There have been incidents where Queer people have been discriminated against in courtroom proceedings, having their sexual lives exploited and made courtroom fodder. Lesbian defendants especially have been mired in hate speech from prosecutors who defile their orientation and regress into conflated binary arguments regarding masculinity and femininity. As Chapter 4 points out, 20 percent of court employees have reported hearing derogatory comments about sexual orientation that were often made by judges and lawyers. One of the major issues within the courtroom are cases involving what has come to be known as gay or trans panic defenses in which a defendant makes the claim that they harmed the victim because the victim made unsolicited sexual advances towards them. This relates to the discussion in Chapter 2 about the criminalization of queerness as related to "imitation" or "deception" and in turn often impacts transgender victims significantly.

Chapter 4 will also explore hate crime legislation and its effects on victimization and sentencing. This certainly is a topic rife with debate as the definitions of what constitutes a hate crime can be vague and certainly most difficult to prove, and the utility of hate crime legislation has been hotly contested. Further, as noted with the lack of trust that Queer people have in the criminal legal system as a whole, there is no guarantee that hate crime victimization will be reported or, if it is, that it will be given the attention it requires.

In Chapter 5, *Queer criminology and corrections*, we discuss what happens once Queer offenders are adjudicated, tried, and punished. This chapter examines the world of corrections and how that relates to punishment. We explore the ways in which correctional officers and institutions treat LGBTQ individuals within both adult and juvenile facilities and how that often-discriminatory treatment can have long-lasting effects on them. Again, we will examine issues within corrections both in the United States and abroad and detail the experiences that Queer people face beyond their initial sentences. For instance, we explore the additional punishments they are met with upon their incarceration, such as increased victimization and rape, and the state's inability to assess their unique safety requirements beyond isolating Queer offenders: an action that can have long-lasting emotional and psychological effects, and that can be argued is a violation of the Eighth Amendment's cruel and unusual punishment provisions. This speaks to the problems associated with housing and classifying Queer incarcerated populations including juveniles in youth facilities who also face an increase of victimization. This chapter will also detail policy implementations and implications since the passing of the Prison Rape Elimination Act of 2003.

Transgender men and women have special needs when it comes to their physical and psychological well-being, and this should make no difference when it comes to inmates. Therefore, this chapter will highlight medical provisions and the right to transition debate that has been in the media recently, especially since the recent case of transgender Massachusetts inmate, Michelle Kosilek. Also, this chapter notes that correctional officers, much like police officers, who identify as LGBTQ have experienced harassment and discrimination as well. Chapter 5 will highlight several instances of discrimination on the job; moreover, special attention will be given to a transidentified male-to-female correctional officer working in what has been defined as one of the United States' toughest prisons, California's San Quentin. Her story is unique and eye-opening with regard to how both the inmates and her supervisors and coworkers responded to her transition.

In the final chapter, *Future directions in queer criminology*, we will revisit these topics and make suggestions for why there continues to be a need for queer criminology and why there is an importance for queer criminology to be recognized within the world of critical criminology. The final chapter will explore the importance of developing and implementing a queer criminology and how this exploration and implementation is paramount when examining the criminal legal system as a means to control groups of people and individuals who identify outside of the heteronormative landscape.

Throughout this book, we argue that queer criminology is more than simply adding sexuality or gender identity as independent variables to research (i.e. the "add Queer and stir" approach). Instead, as the chapters will indicate, we provide our readers with an array of examples from the United States and beyond that highlight the ways in which sexuality and gender are used as weapons of the state to control the behavior of those who do not fit the societal norm. As you progress through this book, we ask you to consider these questions: What does a queer criminology look like to you? What would the theoretical constructions be? Is there a specific queer methodology to conducting research? These are questions that may not have definitive answers as of today. However, it is important that we continue to explore these inquiries, and we offer this book as a contribution to that conversation.

References

Adler, F. 1975. *Sisters in crime: The rise of the new female criminal.* New York, NY: McGraw-Hill.

Ball, M. 2014a. *What's queer about queer criminology?* In D. Peterson & V. Panfil (eds.), *Handbook of LGBT communities, crime, and justice* (pp. 531–555). New York, NY: Springer.

Ball, M. 2014b. *Queer criminology, critique, and the "art of not being governed."* Critical Criminology, *22*, (1): 21–34.

Belknap, J. & Holsinger, K. 1998. *An overview of delinquent girls: How theory and practice failed and the need for innovative change.* In R. Zaplin (ed.), *Female crime and delinquency: Critical perspectives and effective interventions* (pp. 31–64). Gaithersburg, MD: Aspen.

Belknap, J. & Holsinger, K. 2006. *The gendered nature of risk factors for delinquency.* Feminist Criminology, *1*, (1): 48–71.

Brennan, T., Breitenbach, M., & Dieterich, W. 2010. *Unraveling women's pathways to serious crime: New findings and links to feminist prior pathways.* American Probation and Parole Association.

Brightman, S., Lenning, E., & McElrath, K. 2015. *State-directed sterilizations in North Carolina: Victim-centeredness and Reparations.* British Journal of Criminology, *55*, (3): 474–493.

Buist, C.L. & Stone, C. 2014. *Transgender victims and offenders: Failures of the United States criminal justice system and the necessity of queer criminology*. Critical Criminology, *22*, (1): 35–47.

Butler, J. 1990. *Gender trouble*. New York, NY: Routledge.

Chesney-Lind, M. 1988. *Doing feminist criminology*. The Criminologist, *13*, (4): 16–17.

Daly, K. 1992. *Women's pathway to felony court: Feminist theories of lawbreaking and problems of representation*. Southern California Review of Law and Women's Studies, *2*: 11–52.

Department of Justice. 2015. *Investigation of the Ferguson Police Department*. Washington, DC: United States Department of Justice Civil Rights Division.

Doyon, J.A. 2014. *Corporate environmental crime in the electronic waste industry: The case of Executive Recycling, Inc. Internet Journal of Criminology: Critical Perspectives on Green Criminology Series*: 68–89.

Ferrell, J. 2013. *Cultural criminology and the politics of meaning*. Critical Criminology, *21*, (3): 257–271.

Foucault, M. 1980. *Power/knowledge: Selected interviews and other writings*. New York, NY: Pantheon Press.

Green, A.I. 2007. *Queer theory and sociology: Locating the subject and the self in sexuality studies*. Sociological Theory, *25*, (1): 26–45.

Groombridge, N. 1998. *Perverse criminologies: The closet of Doctor Lombroso*. Social and Legal Studies, *8*, (4): 531–548.

Hagan, J., Simpson, J., & Gillis, A.R. 1987. *Class in the household: A power-control theory of gender and delinquency*. American Journal of Sociology, *92*, (4): 788–816.

Jagose, A. 1996. *Queer theory: An introduction*. New York, NY: New York University Press.

Kirsch, M.N. 2000. *Queer theory and social change*. New York, NY: Routledge.

Kramer, R.C. & Bradshaw, E.A. 2011. *US state crimes related to nuclear weapons: Is there hope for change in the Obama administration*. International Journal of Comparative and Applied Criminal Justice, *35*, (3): 243–259.

Leighton, P. 2010. *A professor of white collar crime reviews USA's* White Collar *series*. The Critical Criminologist, *19*, (4): 8–16.

Lenning, E. 2009. *Beyond the binary: Exploring the dimensions of gender orientation and representation*. International Journal of Social Inquiry, *2* (2): 39–54.

Lynch, M.J. & Michalowski, R. 2000. *Primer in radical criminology: Critical perspectives on crime, power, and identity*. New York, NY: Criminal Justice Press.

Mallicoat, S.L. 2015. *Women and crime*. Thousand Oaks, CA: Sage.

Mogul, J.L., Ritchie, A., & Whitlock, K. 2011. *Queer (in)justice: The criminalization of LGBT people in the United States*. Boston, MA: Beacon Press.

Peterson, D. & Panfil, V.R. (eds.) 2014a. *Handbook of LGBT communities, crime, and justice*. New York, NY: Springer.

Peterson, D. & Panfil, V.R. 2014b. *Introduction: Reducing the invisibility of sexual and gender identities in criminology and criminal justice*. In Peterson, D. & Panfil, V.R. (eds.) *Handbook of LGBT communities, crime, and justice* (pp. 3–14). New York, NY: Springer.

Prison Rape Elimination Act of 2003. PREA Public Law, 108–79. Accessed from http://www.gpo.gov/fdsys/pkg/PLAW-108publ79/pdf/PLAW-108publ79.pdf.

Rutter, V. & Schwartz, P. 2012. *The gender of sexuality: Exploring sexual possibilities*. Lanham, MD: Rowen & Littlefield.

Sedgwick, E. 1990. *Epistemology of the closet*. Berkeley, CA: University of California Press.

Simon, R.J. 1975. *Women and crime*. Lexington, MA: Lexington Books.

Tomsen, S. 1997. *Was Lombroso queer? Criminology, criminal justice, and the heterosexual imaginary*. Sydney, Australia: Hawkins Press, Australian Institute of Criminology.

West, C. & Zimmerman, D.H. 1987. *Doing gender. Gender & Society, 1*, (2): 125–151.

Woods, J.B. 2014. *Queer contestations and the future of a critical "queer" criminology. Critical Criminology, 22*, (1): 5–19.

Woods, J.B. 2015. *The birth of modern criminology and gendered constructions of the homosexual criminal identity. Journal of Homosexuality, 62*: 131–166.

2

CRIMINALIZING QUEERNESS

Throughout history and across the globe, Queer people have had their bodies regulated, been arrested, and have faced punishment for no other reason than their sexual and gender identities and behaviors. Quite literally, their "queerness" has been criminalized. While subsequent chapters will focus on specific instances of discrimination and violence against Queer people by and within law enforcement, courts, and correctional institutions around the world, in this chapter, we focus on the much broader historical and contemporary context within which those acts are situated. Today, billions of people live in countries where homosexual sex and, in some cases, the mere mention of homosexuality is outlawed. In the United States, antisodomy laws were in place until 2003 (see *Lawrence v. Texas*), but similar laws persist around the globe and citizens in the United States continue to be affected by legislation of the past. An even greater number of people live in countries where gender non-conformity is policed, prosecuted, and punished. It is the pervasive proscription of queer bodies, behaviors, and rights that make criminal legal systems around the world the primary institutions through which queerness is socially controlled, thus demanding the attention of queer criminology.

Criminalizing homosexuality

Nearly half (78) of the countries around the world have laws prohibiting the mere act of *consensual* sex between members of the same sex, at least five of which impose the punishment of death (Csete & Cohen 2010; Human Rights Watch 2008; Itaborahy & Zhu 2014; Ottosson 2008). Though these laws vary in terms of the language used to define illegal sex, the severity of punishment for violating them, and the degree to which they are enforced, they all *appear* to stem from and promote a global culture of homophobia and a forced value of compulsory heterosexuality. In truth, however, these laws (as pervasive as they may be) did not at the time of their implementation inherently or necessarily reflect a global culture. A significant portion of them reflected colonial British values and not necessarily the values of the countries now left to enforce them. Indeed, no less than 40 colonies and countries in Asia, the Pacific, and Africa have or had antisodomy laws imposed on them by British rulers seeking to "inculcate European morality into resistant masses" (Human Rights Watch 2008: 5). Ireland (2013) found that there was in fact a causal relationship between British colonialism and contemporary African antihomosexuality laws, and that it was more significant than a country's religiosity or authoritarian political leadership. Combined, however, these variables are even more predictive; today, antihomosexuality rhetoric and laws are often used to distract the religious public's attention from corrupt leadership (Ireland 2013; M'Baye 2013).

While it cannot be said that no homophobia existed in Africa prior to colonialism, it is believed that colonialism exasperated any that did exist and was certainly the reason that homophobia became state-sponsored (Human Rights Watch 2008; Ireland 2013). Today, many Africans staunchly believe that homosexuality was imported from the West, so determining how accepted or practiced homosexuality was or was not prior to colonization is challenging and further complicated by the fact that many of the words used to describe homosexuality were actually imported from the West (Epprecht 1998). Nevertheless, evidence of same-sex relations in Africa can be traced all the way back to drawings by Bushmen, are well documented by anthropologists, and were often described by colonialists

as consensual (M'Baye 2013; Msibi 2011). So, while there is no indi-
cation that these acts were celebrated prior to colonization, neither is
there to suggest that homosexuality was any more than ignored in a
"don't ask, don't tell" fashion (Epprecht 1998; Msibi 2011).

Prior to institutionalizing homophobia in Africa, Britain first
imported sodomy laws (modeled after their own) into India in 1860
with Section 377 of the Indian Penal Code, which criminalizes
homosexual sex and imposes sentences of up to life in prison (Human
Rights Watch 2008). Section 377 then became the model for antisodomy laws in a host of other British colonies. Thus, the twisted reality
is that many of the antisodomy laws that stain Africa and the rest of
the globe were not necessarily about each country's individual desire
to criminalize homosexual sex, but rather about Britain using a country's own criminal legal system to import imperialism. Regardless
of the origins of the laws, however, they have persisted and serve to
breed and promote a contemporary culture of heteronormativity and
violent homophobia around the world.

On our way to the police station, the police officers insulted
us and beat us with batons on our heads and bodies. They kept
saying they were going to burn us for being dirty pedes [fag-
gots]. . . . The next morning they began to question us about
our homosexuality, and on Tuesday, they took us to Channel
Two and to Cameroon Radio and Television. They paraded us
on the news saying the police had dismantled a network of
homosexuals.

Christian, Cameroon
Human Rights Watch 2010a: 2

Antigay laws are undoubtedly most prominent in Africa, with
homosexuality (not necessarily limited to sodomy) being illegal in 38
African countries. Though official data on arrests for homosexuality
is inaccessible or even nonexistent, a plethora of anecdotal evidence

suggests that African gays and lesbians are in constant fear and danger of arrest and prosecution, often despite any concrete evidence of their homosexuality. In Cameroon, for example, gays and lesbians are arrested by the dozens in establishments suspected to be gay bars and are even arrested in their own homes based on lists of "presumed" homosexuals published in local newspapers or merely on the suspicions of family and neighbors. In one such case in 2006, four young women were arrested for lesbianism – the only evidence of which being a "tip" from the grandmother of one of the girls. They were each sentenced to three years of probation (Human Rights Watch 2010a). More recently, in 2011, well-known Ugandan gay rights activist David Kato was bludgeoned to death in his home after winning an injunction against the Ugandan newspaper *Rolling Stone*, which had published his address and picture on a list of "Top Homosexuals" under a headline that read "Hang Them" (Rice 2011; Walsh 2011).

Just because a country has an antisodomy law does not necessarily mean that it is enforced with the same tenacity as other laws. Though same-sex relations are illegal in Kenya, for example, there are very few convictions under the law. Nevertheless, the sentiment of the law does promote a homophobic culture, and consequently, LGBTI citizens report widespread police harassment, abuse, and corruption (Finerty 2013; Kenya Human Rights Commission 2011). A study conducted by the Kenya Human Rights Commission (2011) revealed that LGBTI citizens, especially gay male sex workers, are frequently arrested on fabricated charges, or are forced to pay bribes or have sex with officers to avoid them. One Kenyan doctor described having to pay a bribe of 100,000 shillings (approximately $1,000 USD) to avoid being paraded naked in front of his neighbors and the local media before being arrested. Another victim of police violence described being raped at an officer's home when he was unable to come up with a bail of 500 shillings. The rape was unprotected and he contracted gonorrhea. Without a doubt, these instances are made possible through the fear and stigma caused by Kenya's antihomosexuality laws. Officials are keenly aware that victims are unlikely to report or challenge abuse and humiliation.

In addition to the harassment and brutality described above, homosexual acts remain punishable by death in Iran, Yemen, Saudi

Arabia, Mauratania, Sudan, and parts of Africa's most populated country, Nigeria (Itaborahy & Zhu 2014). While reports of citizens being sentenced to death in these countries surface frequently, news of actual executions rarely make it to the mainstream. The exception to this is Iran, where NGOs and alternative news sources have reported multiple executions for *lavat* (the Sharia term for sodomy) in the past decade. To name a few instances, at least two men were hanged in 2005 (Human Rights Watch 2005), at least three more were hanged in 2011 (Dehghan 2011), two were hanged in March 2014 (Kredo 2014), and still at least two more were hanged in August 2014 (Michaelson 2014). It is safe to assume that executions for *lavat* occur much more frequently than we are aware, since trials regarding moral violations are often held in secret and the Iranian government limits what the press reveals in order to avoid global scrutiny for its public and frequent use of the death penalty in general (Human Rights Watch 2010b).

As briefly mentioned at the onset, the United States is thought to have moved past criminalizing homosexuality via the 2003 landmark Supreme Court case of *Texas v. Lawrence*. The defendant, John Lawrence, was prosecuted in 1998 for violating a Texas law regarding "homosexual conduct" when the police entered his home (for a supposed weapons incident) and discovered him engaging in consensual sex with another man. Lawrence appealed his conviction and the Supreme Court declared the Texas law to be a violation of the constitutional right to privacy. The ruling was considered by and large to be a sweeping victory for the gay rights movement, but the effects of sodomy-related laws continue to haunt the Queer community throughout the United States.

One case in point is in the state of Louisiana, where the state's crimes against nature (CAN) statute was expanded to include solicitation for the purpose of prostitution. The expanded law required those prosecuted to register as a sex offender for 15 years. To be clear, there are laws against solicitation for prostitution in Louisiana that are separate from the CAN expansion. Those prosecuted under the solicitation laws (a misdemeanor), however, did not face the consequence of registering, as did those charged with a felony under the CAN law. In her role as Director of the *Sex Workers Project* at the

Urban Justice Center, Andrea Ritchie (2013) discovered that, unsurprisingly, those charged under the CAN law were by and large gay men of color and transgender women. She also found that in certain regions, Black women were disproportionately affected by the CAN laws – for example, of all the CAN-related registered sex offenders in Orleans Parish in 2011, 75 percent were women and 80 percent were Black (Ritchie 2013).

The result of the Louisiana law and those similar to it can be devastating, as most of the convicted were impoverished to begin with and now face even greater economic strain in light of fees for registering (hundreds of dollars) and the even greater difficulty of gaining employment while registered as a sex offender. Ritchie (2013: 369) describes how this sort of injustice sets the stage for the experiences and impact of intersectionality we outline in subsequent chapters when she notes that "[b]eyond such explicit policing of racialized gender, individuals perceived to be transgressing racialized gender norms are consciously or subconsciously framed as both inherently 'disorderly' and profoundly sexualized." Though massive organizing and legal protest resulted in the elimination of the registration requirement of the Louisiana CAN law, Queer people, particularly those of color, continue to face gendered, racialized, and sexualized profiling by law enforcement, a direct result of centuries of dehumanizing and criminalizing queerness.

Despite the pervasiveness of antisodomy laws around the world and especially in Africa, there have been calls to repeal them, including from United Nations Secretary-General Ban Ki-Moon, former Secretary of State Hillary Clinton, and, ironically, British Prime Minister David Cameron (Kretz 2013). The push to decriminalize homosexuality, however, concerns even some members of the Queer community (especially in African countries) because the threat of backlash is so palpable. In particular, there are concerns that decriminalization will result in discrimination and physical violence against the Queer community beyond what already exists. African citizens overwhelmingly disapprove of homosexuality and many believe that there would not be homosexuality in Africa if it were not for Western influences and colonization (Kretz 2013). This seems a rather counterintuitive attitude given the origin of the sodomy laws, but nevertheless, it creates a homophobic climate conducive to violent backlash in the wake of any decriminalization measure interpreted to be some form of contemporary colonization.

Indeed, the United States did experience a wave of antigay backlash after *Lawrence v. Texas* (2003) decriminalized gay sex. In the year immediately following the decision, 11 states introduced constitutional amendments defining marriage as between cisgender men and women, and then President George W. Bush announced his support for a federal constitutional amendment. In 2006, eight more states introduced constitutional bans on gay marriage. It wasn't until 2008 that public attitudes and state laws began to shift in favor of equality, and today, as of June 26, 2015, all 50 states have marriage equality (see post-script). In hindsight, the immediate backlash may have paved the way for this change in momentum.

It is too early for a victory dance, however, as US states continue to consider anti-LGBTQ legislation. Most recently, several states have adopted or introduced "Religious Freedom Restoration Acts" (mirrored after the federal Act of the same name), some of which would or do allow public and private servants to deny Queer citizens assistance based on religious objections to homosexuality and gender nonconformity. Even as we write this, Indiana's governor, Mike Pence, has passed the Religious Freedom Restoration Act, which will go into effect on July 1, 2015. The legislation has raised concerns from the Queer community, who have indicated that while this law does not make specific mention of discriminatory practices, it effectively condones discrimination based on an individual's religious beliefs. Indiana is the twentieth state to enact legislation such as this in recent years. However, Indiana's law differs in that some other states with religious freedom laws also have separate antidiscrimination clauses that protect gays and lesbians. Indiana does not offer protections to gays and lesbians, but it does have provisions that protect sex and race. Thus, business owners in Indiana cannot use the racist traditions of religion to deny a Black customer, but they could use their religious beliefs to deny service to Queer customers.

So, what would a bill like this mean to a Queer person in Indiana – quite simply put, imagine that you are eating lunch at the counter of a local restaurant, and between your bites of burger, the owner asks you to leave. You ask why and the owner replies that they don't serve "your kind" – your kind meaning, gay. If this sounds familiar to you, it should, because it happened countless times in US history, culminating in what has come to be known as the "Woolworth Lunch Counter" incident of 1960 when several young Black men sat down to eat at a Woolworth's in North Carolina and were denied service because they were Black. The young men refused to leave the restaurant and their sit-in sparked a six-month-long protest that ultimately led to the desegregation of the Woolworth lunch counter in July of 1960. Fifty-five years later, here we are again, for if you are gay and in Indiana in July, this similar bigotry could happen to you. Time will only tell if the same sort of protests will occur that may ultimately impact this legislation.

Several states also have laws limiting pro-LGBTQ speech in education, particularly as it relates to sex education. Arizona state law, for example, prohibits sex educators from promoting a "homosexual lifestyle" or suggesting that safe sex is even an option for homosexuals. Legal scholars argue that these laws, dubbed "no promo homo" laws, are the relics of a larger struggle between the *politics of recognition* (i.e. Queers fighting for equality) and the *politics of preservation* (i.e. conservatives fighting to preserve "family values") – identity politics playing out through rhetoric and legal battles (Eskridge 2000). Eskridge (2000: 1376) argues that the "state-supported closet" created by these sorts of laws "chills individual self-expression and political participation by GLBT people." No doubt, this is why in some parts of the world special interest groups have successfully lobbied to make it illegal to even express one's support of gay rights.

Perhaps the most recent example of this is Russia's "gay propaganda law," which makes it a crime to promote homosexuality to minors – in other words, it is illegal to speak to minors about homosexuality in any way that is not disparaging. The law's enforcement has resulted in at least four guilty convictions, including the arrests and prosecution of two demonstrators, Alexei Kiselyov and Kirill Nepomnyashy, whose crimes were holding signs that read "Gay is Normal" (Human Rights Watch 2014a; *St. Petersburg Times* 2012). Given the cultural climate towards the Queer community in Russia, no doubt confounded by the new law, it is no surprise that 2012 saw a surge of anti-LGBTQ vigilante groups such as *Occupy Pedophilia*, founded by neo-Nazi Maxim Martisinkevich. *Occupy Pedophilia* and similar vigilante groups have kidnapped, detained, sexually abused, and humiliated gay men and teenagers for the purpose of exposing them through videos of the encounters that are subsequently posted on YouTube. One victim of a vigilante group said that "[t]hey [vigilantes] think they have the right to treat us like this. I feel as if I'm not protected by law. All these bandits have been given impunity" (Human Rights Watch 2014a: 34). The criminal behavior of *Occupy Pedophilia* has recently been detailed in the HBO documentary *Hunted: The War Against Gays in Russia*. Filmmaker Ben Steele notes that, after filming a scene where the members of the hate group entrap a gay man and film his harassment and abuse, he felt as though his presence prevented the man from being even more violently attacked. Further, Steele comments that the victim was "adamant that he didn't want me to take that material to the police" (Home Box Office 2014). Despite the fact that Russian law could allow for these crimes to be prosecuted as hate crimes, efforts to do so have been thwarted as a result of both the vagueness of the law and the indifference of the Russian criminal legal system. Meanwhile, Russian citizens publicly supporting Queer rights face termination from their jobs and LGBTQ rights groups and Queer events face constant threat of being protested, bombed, or attacked by mobs organized through social groups on the Internet.

Unsurprisingly, these propaganda laws have become a way for some countries to widen the net, so to speak, in terms of criminalizing sexuality. This has been the case in Nigeria, where the arrests and prosecutions for homosexuality have increased since President Goodluck Jonathan signed a law banning gay and lesbian public displays of affection, same-sex marriage (14-year sentence), and membership in gay rights groups (10-year sentence). Even though sodomy has been illegal in Nigeria since British rule, the law was rarely enforced. Jonathan's broader antigay law, however, has resulted in dozens of arrests, including a man allegedly arrested for sending a text message in which he declared his love for another man (Bowcott 2014). As recently as January 2015, 12 men suspected of homosexuality were arrested at an event alleged by the police to be a gay wedding (Dede 2015).

As of this writing, nine countries either outlaw or have proposed to outlaw "gay propaganda" – all having been introduced or implemented in the past two years (Itaborahy & Zhu 2014). One of these proposals has been put forth in Kyrgyzstan, which is considering a gay propaganda law that is even stricter than Russia's and would consider *any* information about the Queer community, regardless of the age of the audience, to be propaganda (Verbenko 2014). Thus, the global struggle for Queer rights and recognition has not been a linear journey – rather, it has been marked by a constant series of advances and setbacks.

A looming contemporary dilemma in regards to the persistent criminalization of Queerness is the unwillingness of many states to uphold their own laws and/or a disjuncture between the domestic laws of nation-states and their international legal obligations. A perfect example of this is the previously mentioned violence experienced by Queer individuals and organizations in Russia. The Russian constitution does protect freedom of expression and protects citizens from discrimination, though clearly its application is inequitable. It is when states fail to uphold their own laws that international statutes become applicable, so one would presume that Russia's actions (or inactions, rather) would be addressed by any international legal statutes it has committed itself to. However, even though Russia has signed and ratified the *International Covenant on Civil and Political Rights* (ICCPR), which expressly requires states to allow for freedom of expression and experience equal treatment under the law, Queer citizens and their allies are seemingly exempt. And even though the UN Human Rights Committee has ruled against Russia in one case of prosecuting someone for violation of the "gay propaganda" law and the UN Committee on Torture has urged Russia to work towards protecting its Queer citizens from discrimination and violence, the state does not appear to be heeding that decision or advice by making any tangible changes. Further, as exemplified in filmmaker Steele's comments, the victims of violence and torment at the hands of antigay militants in Russia are too fearful to report their victimization and there is no evidence to suggest that this is not true for other gay victims around the globe.

Similarly, Iran has effectively skirted the reach of international law by keeping much of its legal process shrouded in secrecy. Like Russia,

Iran has also signed and ratified the ICCPR, which prohibits countries with the death penalty from using it for anything other than the "most serious crimes" – a term that is never defined, thus being subject to interpretation. Additionally, the ICCPR prohibits the death penalty for juveniles. Consensual gay and lesbian sex is punishable by the death penalty in Iran – on the first offense for men and on the fourth for women (after sentences of 100 lashes for the first three offenses) – a punishment that Human Rights Watch (2010b) insists has been meted out to Iranian citizens, including people who committed offenses as juveniles. Though these and other countries have been criticized and ruled against by international legal bodies, the effects seem to be symbolic, minor, or nonexistent.

It is true that, in comparison to other "criminal acts," consensual homosexual sex is rarely prosecuted, and punishment for propaganda is rarer still. Nevertheless, even if laws against same-sex relationships are antiquated and seldom prosecuted, if they exist, then individuals can still be detained and/or arrested and charged, prosecuted, and punished all based on the discretion of the authorities in that particular location (Csete & Cohen 2010). Ultimately, these laws (regardless of how often they are applied) legitimize homophobic attitudes and perpetuate interpersonal and institutional violence against the Queer community and certainly lend credence to the fear that Queer folks have regarding all arms of the criminal legal system, as highlighted by the experiences of transgender and gender nonconforming individuals around the world.

Criminalizing gender nonconformity

Though laws governing queer behavior vary across the globe, laws regarding the "impersonation" of the opposite sex seem to be far-reaching and surprisingly commonplace. Throughout history and even in recent years, transgender individuals around the world have been harassed by law enforcement, arrested, charged, and prosecuted specifically because of or as a result of their gender presentation, including in the United States, Kuwait, Malaysia, Israel, and the United Kingdom, among others (Dwyer 2011; Gross 2009; Human Rights Watch 2012; Human Rights Watch 2014a).

These cases sometimes arise when a cisgender individual (often female) discovers that her or his romantic partner is transgender (often a transmale) and claims that the sex was only consensual because she or he thought the "offender" was a biological male (or female). One of the more recent cases was heard in the United Kingdom in 2013, where a 13-year-old transgender boy named Scott McNally pursued a three-year online relationship with a 12-year-old girl. After three years of online interaction the two met and engaged in sexual activity in 2011 – McNally was 17 and the other child was 16 at the time. Upon learning of McNally's biological sex, the "victim" claimed that had she known Scott was biologically female, she would not have consented to sex. Ultimately the courts agreed that the interactions between the two constituted rape by deception, and McNally pleaded guilty to six charges of assault. He was convicted to three years in a juvenile facility and a lifetime on the sex offender registry (Dixon 2013). Not surprisingly, McNally was vilified by the media, referred to as Justine (his birth name) and said to have "fooled the 16-year-old and her family and friends with her disguise" and "lured her into intimate encounters, promising her marriage and children" (Dixon 2013). In their study of the media depiction of transgender murder victims, Shilt and Westbrook (2009) found this "deception" frame to be present 56 percent of the time. So, whether represented as an offender or a victim, it is the trans person's gender presentation that is framed as the problem, not transphobia.

It must be pointed out that what is unique about McNally's case is that the defendant and the plaintiff were close in age, and their relationship was not in violation of the UK's age of consent laws. To the contrary, the majority of "rape by deception" cases do appear to include the violation of age of consent laws, often proving to be a convenient way to punish gender nonconformity. Such was the case for Chris Wilson, a Scottish transgender man who allegedly had sexual relations with two teenage girls – one of whom said she was 16, the age of consent – when he was 20 years old. Wilson told her that he was 17 years old. He was sentenced to 240 hours of community service and placed on the sex offender registry. Interestingly, even though his alleged offense was statutory rape, he was not charged with such. Rather, he was charged with sexual intimacy by fraud, which suggests his conviction was, like McNally, about his gender identity and not about concern for his "victims." As in McNally's case, the media coverage of Wilson's case didn't focus on sexual assault so much as it did his gender identity. The BBC (2013) ran the headline "Sex fraud woman put on probation" for a story about "a woman who posed as a man" – though the article claimed that Chris had lived as a male since childhood, the author consistently used female pronouns.

Alex Sharpe, a Professor of Law at Keele University, makes an excellent point about the implicit double standard that characterizes cases like McNally's and Wilson's – bias that we wouldn't see if the "offender" represented other marginalized groups, such as racial minorities. She points out that no court of law would convict a light-skinned, mixed-race person of rape by deception if the white person that she or he had sex with became outraged and felt "violated" upon learning of the individual's mixed race background (Sharpe 2013). The cases described here are undoubtedly about the policing and punishment of gender nonconformity and not about the protection of "innocent victims" from deceit or sexual assault.

Some would argue that these cases, while obviously related to the gender presentation of the defendants, would not have been pursued had the individuals not been sexually involved. Though this may be true, there are many examples globally where transgender individuals have faced mistreatment and abuse by law enforcement, arrest, and punishment for no other reason than the clothing they wear or their gendered mannerisms. This occurred historically in the United States and continues to occur around the world, as described below. Indeed, as will be detailed in the proceeding chapter, the case of Brandon Teena in the United States is a prime example of how transgender people have been victimized by agents of the criminal legal system and how the law has done little to protect their rights.

Though most US anti-Queer laws of the past were largely used to regulate the behavior of gay men, it was butch lesbians who were often the victims of "cross-dressing" laws (Eskridge 1997). Both California and New York had laws against wearing a disguise or "masquerading" in public, and the city of Miami, Florida, outlawed impersonating a female and "dress not customarily worn by his or her sex" (Eskridge 1997: 723). Toledo, Ohio, Chicago, Illinois, and other cities across the country had similar statutes (Mogul, Ritchie, & Whitlock 2011). Neither of the two state laws was exclusively meant to address gender nonconformity, but those arrested were frequently lesbians wearing traditionally male clothing. The purported general guideline that law enforcement officers in New York used was that the individual had to be wearing at least three articles of clothing that matched the "offenders" biological sex. Many of the "cross-dressing" arrests were made as part of larger "antihomosexual" raids of popular gay hangouts in the 1950s. Twelve female patrons, for example, were arrested for "mannish dress" during a 1957 vice raid of Jimmie White's Tavern in Tampa, Florida (Eskridge 1997). As will be discussed in Chapter 3, however, these raids are not simply relics of the past.

Though these antiquated laws were eventually removed from the books, trans people across the United States are still arrested for their appearance, often under the guise of solicitation offenses. This is exactly what happened to Arizona State University student Monica Jones, a transgender woman of color who was arrested in 2013 and convicted of "manifesting prostitution," which is to say she was interacting with passengers in cars (Kellaway 2015). Though Jones's conviction was overturned in January of 2015, trans women (especially trans women of color) face constant threat of harassment and arrest by police – a phenomena so common that it has been dubbed "walking while trans." A report released by the National Center for Transgender Equality in 2011 revealed that 22 percent of the 6,456 transgender and gender nonconforming respondents had experienced harassment by police, with Black respondents reporting the highest rate of harassment (38%) and whites the lowest (18%). Of those who had experienced harassment, 6 percent had been physically assaulted and 2 percent had been sexually assaulted by law enforcement officers (Grant, Mottet, & Tanis 2011). While some who reported harassment were sex workers, many were not, suggesting that "walking while trans" is a very real danger for those who challenge traditional gender norms, regardless of the context of their interaction with law enforcement.

While law enforcement in the United States must now find creative ways (i.e. solicitation laws) to arrest people for their gender nonconformity, laws similar to the old masquerade laws of the United States are still found in other countries today, including Kuwait and Malaysia.

Every time they catch me they expect me to repent. If I wear women's clothes, I get caught. If I wear men's clothes, I get caught. If I wear something in between, I get caught. And in all these situations I get sexually harassed. You begin to understand that getting arrested becomes part of your everyday life.

Ghadeer, Kuwait
Human Rights Watch 2012: 34

In 2007, Kuwait amended an older public nuisance law to allow the punishment (of up to one year in prison) of anyone "imitating the opposite sex in any way" (Human Rights Watch 2012: 1). Not only does the law not specify what constitutes "imitating" but, since there is no means to legally change one's sex in Kuwait, the law also affects individuals who have undergone sex reassignment surgery. Not surprisingly, the law ushered in police abuse towards transgender women, and led to their being arrested when approaching police to report other crimes. The law has amplified public scrutiny of trans women, and that heightened awareness has led ordinary citizens and health-care workers to purposely report trans women that they see in public or find themselves treating. Transgender women also report crimes being committed against them primarily because the perpetrator knows that if she reports the offense, she'll be charged with imitation. A woman named Haneen described to Human Rights Watch (2012) how her rapist literally drove her to a patrol car and dared her to get out of his vehicle and report the brutal attack against her.

They were rough. One of them squeezed my breasts. I was completely humiliated. . . . They stripped me completely naked. One of them took a police baton and poked at my genitals. Everyone was looking – the men [Religious Department officials] as well as the women. They took photos of my naked body.

Victoria, Malaysia
Human Rights Watch 2014b: 27

In Malaysia, transgender citizens, especially trans women, face prosecution and incarceration for "cross-dressing" under Sharia law (Human Rights Watch 2014b). Though the laws vary by state in Malaysia, prison sentences for "posing" as someone of the opposite sex can range from six months to three years and can result in fines as much as a month's worth of salary. According to Human Rights Watch (2014b), the Islamic departments that enforce Sharia law often do so with the assistance of civil officers. The individuals arrested are given no representation in Islamic courts and, unsurprisingly, are usually found guilty.

Interestingly, antigay and antitransgender laws and sentiments are not entwined in all countries. In India, where homosexuality is punishable by incarceration, being transgender is now a legally protected status (Sampath 2015). Transgender and intersex individuals, long referred to in India as *hijra*, have recently been given the right to identify as *hijra* on all government documents. Now nearly half a million Indian citizens will be recognized as members of the third sex. In keeping with the country's overall homophobic climate, however, the law was very specific to note that it did not extend to gays, lesbians, or bisexuals.

The examples of criminalized queerness given throughout this chapter provide the context for what is described in the following chapters on law enforcement, legal systems, and corrections. It is widely accepted in criminology that racial minorities, especially in the United States, experience discrimination and disparity in the criminal legal system in large part due to the historical practice of criminalizing and punishing their very existence (e.g. slavery and Jim Crow laws). Indeed, the scars left by racism have proven to be nearly impossible to erase and are most distinctly revealed in the criminal legal system. Thus, it should be no surprise that Queer people, especially Queer people of color, whose sexual behavior and bodies are still criminalized and punished to extreme degrees, have unique and largely negative experiences with and within the criminal legal system.

Recommended viewing

A Jihad for Love, 2007. [Film] Directed by Parvez Sharma. USA: Halal Films.
Before Stonewall, 1984. [Film] Directed by Greta Schiller & Robert Rosenberg. USA: Before Stonewall, Inc.

Born This Way, 2013. [Film] Directed by Shaun Kadlec & Deb Tullmann. USA: The Film Collaborative.

Call Me Kuchu, 2012. [Film] Directed by Katherine Fairfax Wright & Malika Zouhali-Worrall. USA: Cinedigm.

Dangerous Living: Coming Out in the Developing World, 2003. [Film] Directed by John Scagliotti. USA: After Stonewall Productions.

God Loves Uganda, 2013. [Film] Directed by Roger Ross Williams. USA: Full Credit Productions.

Hunted: The War Against Gays In Russia, 2014. [Film] Directed by Ben Steele. USA: HBO.

Paragraph 175, 2000. [Film] Directed by Rob Epstein & Jeffrey Friedman. USA: New Yorker Films.

Screaming Queens: The Riot at Compton's Cafeteria, 2005. [Film] Directed by Victor Silverman & Susan Stryker. USA: Frameline.

Stonewall Uprising, 2010. [Film] Directed by Kate Davis & David Heilbroner. USA: First Run Features.

References

BBC. 2013. *Sex fraud woman put on probation. BBC News*, April 9. Accessed from http://www.bbc.com/news/uk-scotland-north-east-orkney-shetland-22078298.

Bowcott, O. 2014. *Nigeria arrests dozens as anti-gay law comes into force. The Guardian*, January 14. Accessed from http://www.theguardian.com/world/2014/jan/14/nigeria-arrests-dozens-anti-gay-law.

Csete, J. & Cohen, J. 2010. *Health benefits of legal services for criminalized populations: The case of people who use drugs, sex workers and sexual and gender minorities. Journal of Law, Medicine & Ethics, 38*, (4): 816–831.

Dede, S. 2015. *12 homosexuals arrested in Kano gay wedding. Pulse*, January 27. Accessed from http://pulse.ng/gist/caught-in-the-act-12-homosexuals-arrested-in-kano-gay-wedding-id3437582.html.

Dehghan, S.K. 2011. *Iran executes three men on homosexuality charges. The Guardian*, September 7. Accessed from http://www.theguardian.com/world/2011/sep/07/iran-executes-men-homosexuality-charges.

Dixon, H. 2013. *18-year-old woman masqueraded as a boy to get girl in bed. The Telegraph*, March 21. Accessed from http://www.telegraph.co.uk/news/uknews/crime/9946687/18-year-old-woman-masqueraded-as-boy-to-get-girl-into-bed.html.

Dwyer, A. 2011. *"It's not like we're going to jump them": How transgressing heteronormativity shapes police interactions with LGBT young people. Youth Justice, 11*, (3): 203–220.

Epprecht, M. 1998. *The "unsaying" of indigenous homosexualities in Zimbabwe: Mapping a blindspot in an African masculinity. Journal of Southern African Studies, 24*, (4): 631–651.

Eskridge, W. 1997. *Privacy jurisprudence and the apartheid of the closet: 1946–1961. Florida State University Law Review, 24,* (4): 703–838.

Eskridge, W. 2000. *No promo homo: The sedimentation of antigay discourse and the channeling effect of judicial review. New York University Law Review, 75,* (5): 1327–1411.

Finerty, C.E. 2013. *Being gay in Kenya: The implications of Kenya's new constitution for its anti-sodomy laws. Cornell International Law Journal, 45:* 431–459.

Grant, J.M., Mottet, L.A., & Tanis, J. 2011. *Injustice at every turn: A report of the national transgender discrimination survey.* Washington, DC: National Center for Transgender Equality.

Gross, A. 2009. *Gender outlaws before the law: The courts of the borderland. Harvard Journal of Law and Gender, 32,* (1): 165–230.

Home Box Office. 2014. *Hunted: The War Against Gays in Russia.* Interview with Ben Steele. Accessed from http://www.hbo.com/documentaries/hunted-the-war-against-gays-in-russia#/documentaries/hunted-the-war-against-gays-in-russia/interview/ben-steele.html.

Human Rights Watch. 2005. *Iran: Two more executions for homosexual conduct.* Accessed November 22, 2014. Accessed from http://www.hrw.org/news/2005/11/21/iran-two-more-executions-homosexual-conduct.

Human Rights Watch. 2008. *This alien legacy: The origins of "sodomy" laws in British colonialism.* Printed in the United States of America.

Human Rights Watch. 2010a. *Criminalizing identities: Rights abuses in Cameroon based on sexual orientation and gender identity.* Printed in the United States of America.

Human Rights Watch. 2010b. *"We are a buried generation": Discrimination and violence against sexual minorities in Iran.* Printed in the United States of America.

Human Rights Watch. 2012. *"They hunt us down for fun": Discrimination and police violence against transgender women in Kuwait.* Printed in the United States of America.

Human Rights Watch. 2014a. *License to harm: Violence and harassment against LGBT people and activists in Russia.* Printed in the United States of America.

Human Rights Watch. 2014b. *"I'm scared to be a woman": Human rights abuses against transgender people in Malaysia.* Printed in the United States of America.

Ireland, P.R. 2013. *A macro-level analysis of the scope, causes and consequences of homophobia in Africa. African Studies Review, 56,* (2): 47–66.

Itaborahy, L.P. & Zhu, Z. 2014. *State-sponsored homophobia. A world survey of laws: Criminalization, protection & recognition of same-sex love.* Geneva: International Lesbian Gay Bisexual Trans and Intersex Association.

Kellaway, M. 2015. *Arizona appeals court overturns Monica Jones's conviction for "walking while trans." The Advocate,* January 27. Accessed from http://

www.advocate.com/politics/transgender/2015/01/27/arizona-appeals-court-overturns-monica-joness-conviction-walking-whi.

Kenya Human Rights Commission. 2011. *The outlawed among us: A study of the LGBTI community's search for equality and non-discrimination in Kenya.* Nairobi, Kenya: Kenya Human Rights Commission.

Kredo, A. 2014. *Iran executes two for "perversion." The Washington Free Beacon*, March 3. Accessed from http://freebeacon.com/national-security/iran-executes-two-for-perversion/.

Kretz, A.J. 2013. *From "kill the gays" to "kill the gay rights movement": The future of homosexuality legislation in Africa. Journal of International Human Rights, 11*, (2): 207–244.

Lawrence v. Texas. 539 U.S. 558 (2003).

M'Baye, B. 2013. *The origins of Senegalese homophobia: Discourses on homosexuals and transgender people in colonial and postcolonial Senegal. African Studies Review, 56*, (2): 109–128.

Michaelson, J. 2014. *Iran's new gay executions. The Daily Beast*, August 12. Accessed from http://www.thedailybeast.com/articles/2014/08/12/iran-s-new-gay-executions.html.

Mogul, J.L., Ritchie, A., & Whitlock, K. 2011. *Queer (in)justice: The criminalization of LGBT people in the United States.* Boston, MA: Beacon Press.

Msibi, T. 2011. *The lies we have been told: On (homo) sexuality in Africa. Africa Today, 58*, (1): 55–77.

Ottosson, D. 2008. *State-sponsored homophobia: A world survey of laws prohibiting same sex activity between consenting adults.* International Lesbian and Gay Association.

Rice, X. 2011. *Ugandan gay rights activist David Kato found murdered. The Guardian*, January 27. Accessed from http://www.theguardian.com/world/2011/jan/27/ugandan-gay-rights-activist-murdered.

Ritchie, A. 2013. *Crimes against nature: Challenging criminalization of queerness and black women's sexuality. Loyola Journal of Public Interest Law, 14*, (2): 355–374.

Sampath, R. 2015. *India has outlawed homosexuality. But it's better to be transgender there than in the U.S. Washington Post*, January 29. Accessed from http://www.washingtonpost.com/posteverything/wp/2015/01/29/india-has-outlawed-homosexuality-but-its-better-to-be-transgender-there-than-in-the-u-s/.

Schilt, K. & Westbrook, L. 2009. *Doing gender, doing heteronormativity: "Gender normals," transgender people, and the social maintenance of heterosexuality. Gender & Society, 23*, (4): 440–464.

Sharpe, A. 2013. *We must not uphold gender norms at the expense of human dignity: Sexual intimacy, gender variance and criminal law. New Statesmen*, May 1. Accessed from http://www.newstatesman.com/politics/2013/05/we-must-not-uphold-gender-norms-expense-human-dignity.

St. Petersburg Times. 2012. *"Gay is normal" sign gets demonstrators arrested in St. Petersburg*. *St. Petersburg Times*, Issue #1702, April 6. Accessed from http://www.sptimesrussia.com/index.php?action_id=2&story_id=35439.

Verbenko, A. 2014. *Kyrgyzstan follows Russia on "gay propaganda" law*. Institute for War & Peace Reporting, November 10. Accessed from https://iwpr.net/global-voices/kyrgyzstan-follows-russia-gay-propaganda-law.

Walsh, T. 2011. *Ugandan gay rights activist bludgeoned to death*. *CNN*, January 27. Accessed from http://www.cnn.com/2011/WORLD/africa/01/27/uganda.gay.activist.killed/.

3

QUEER CRIMINOLOGY AND LAW ENFORCEMENT

Open any introduction to criminal justice textbook and, in the chapter on law enforcement, you will find a section that highlights the duties of the job. You will most likely find within those same pages discussion on the characteristics of law enforcement officers themselves, and most certainly one, if not the first, characteristic you will learn of is distrust. Officers of the law, namely police officers, distrust the citizens who they are tasked to protect and serve. This is due in large part to the potential dangers of the job and the fear of working in a profession where many of the individuals you encounter are presumed criminals. Certainly this is understandable – as any police officer will tell you, a successful day on the job means that she or he returns home safely at the end of the shift. However, while these suspicions may be justified as a means of self-preservation, these tactics are often used as a means to discriminate against citizens based on, among other characteristics, race, age, gender, or sexual orientation. What is interesting is that these populations who are often the targets of selective enforcement share one salient commonality with the officers who police them – distrust.

At the time of this writing, there is a distinct mistrust of the police amongst minority populations. Police action or inaction resulting in the untimely deaths of Black men across the country has spawned the Internet protest movement #blacklivesmatter (beginning after the murder of Trayvon Martin but increasing in popularity after the shooting death of Michael Brown and the choking death of Eric Garner). While rioters, along with peaceful protestors, have assembled where these events took place and across the country, reliable reporting of just how many Black men and boys are killed by police is not readily available. This can be attributed to unreliable data collection, or the lack of willing participants – for instance, much of the reporting is done voluntarily, and additionally, reports of citizens killed by police are often said to have been done justifiably, which can also be problematic. With that being known, Lee (2014) used Bureau of Justice statistics and US Census data to suggest that Black men are four times more likely to be killed in police custody than white men.

I can't breathe.

Eric Garner
July 17, 2014

What these incidents and data suggest is that minorities (especially Black men) have reason to continue to be suspicious of law enforcement and that officers continue policing the symbolic assailant that historically has been the minority male. The unrest and disdain for police in general may be better documented, and certainly documented more often, with the influence and pervasiveness of the Internet, cell phones, and social media in general, but that doesn't mean that these incidents are new or unique experiences for Black men, as they have long been the targets of police brutality and misconduct. This serves as a constant reminder that their lives are not valued – and are in fact devalued – by law enforcement and the criminal legal system in general. In turn, this behavior also suggests that *white lives do matter* – as victims, as offenders, and as practitioners. The fear that the Black community feels in relation to the police impedes the ability of Black men, women, boys, and girls to obtain human agency; in essence, this fear stifles and blocks the ability of an entire group of people to make their own choices without fear of retribution up to and including death.

We have chosen to highlight the fear that minority populations have of law enforcement and use these recent examples to remind you of the unrest that has been felt. Most of you will recall these events without trouble; you will remember watching the riots that took place in Ferguson, Missouri after the failed indictment of police officer Darren Wilson. You will remember asking why events like this happened in 2014 and continue to persist. You probably saw the hashtag blacklivesmatter come across your Twitter feed or heard about it on the news. What you probably did not know, though, is that three Queer-identified women, Alicia Garza, Patrisse Cullors, and Opal Tometi, created it (Garza 2014). While there is little to no popular news media coverage inundating your front pages, home pages, or Facebook feeds, do not be mistaken – there is a distinct fear that Queer folks, especially trans folks, and even more so trans people of color, have of police officers. Indeed, within the first five weeks of 2015, five trans women of color had been murdered. While police officers were not directly responsible for their deaths, this speaks to the impact of the "matrix of domination" (Collins 2000) and takes into account the many characteristics that impact the intersectionality of oppression. As noted by Crenshaw (1989: 58), who first coined the term, ". . . the intersectional experience is greater than the sum of racism and sexism, any analysis that does not take intersectionality into account cannot sufficiently address the particular manner in which Black women are subordinated." Trans women of color are Black women who have been murdered because of their intersecting identities.

As indicated in Chapter 2, the negative relationship between the police and the Queer community has always existed – the policing of gender variance and the policing of same-sex consensual sex have been used to control the behavior of countless many that have performed gender and sexuality outside of the binary heteronormative lens. While this fractured relationship may have always existed, certainly the Stonewall Riots brought media attention to the malcontent. In what has become an iconic historical event that occurred over four decades ago in the middle of 1969, we see repeated with the continued police harassment of the Queer community. As Mogul, Ritchie, and Whitlock (2011: 46) have noted, as recently as 2003 a primarily Black gay club in Highland Park near Detroit, Michigan, was raided by the local sheriff's department. Hundreds of gays, lesbians, and transgender people were violently detained. Officers made them sit in human waste and they were physically and verbally abused, being called "fags" by officers.

Violence that LGBTQ people have experienced at the hands of law enforcement is an example of our discussion in Chapter 1 on the use of power as a means to oppress and repress the freedoms of others (Foucault 1980). Mogul et al. (2011) also identify the power that police officers have and how that power can influence not only how a particular area is policed, but how being labeled as different can also impact groups of people. In criminology, labeling theory posits that a behavior in and of itself is not deviant or criminal until others begin to define, label, or essentially construct that behavior as such (Becker 1963). Mogul et al. (2011: 49) note

> Social constructions of deviance and criminality pervade the myriad routine practices and procedures through which law enforcement agents decide whom to stop on the streets or highways, whom to question, search, and arrest, and whom to subject to brutal force.

In the forthcoming section, we will discuss in greater detail the experiences of brutality, misconduct and distrust of police officers within the Queer community. We will discuss bias, selective enforcement, and highlight experiences of Queer people in the United States and abroad.

Police brutality and misconduct

It is difficult to objectively define what might be considered police brutality and/or excessive use of force because the events that take place during any given incident are subjectively realized by all different parties involved. With that being said, one broad definition comes from Cao (2003: 1; emphasis in the original) who defines police brutality as "citizens' *judgment* that they have not been treated with full rights and dignity by police as expected in a democratic society."

Thus, behavior from verbal harassment to excessive physical force up to and including unjustifiable shootings may all be considered as misconduct and/or brutality.

In 2010, the CATO Institute's National Police Misconduct Reporting Project found that there were over 4,800 reports of police misconduct that involved over 6,600 sworn law enforcement officers, including over 350 cases that involved administrative or high ranking officers. These incidents of misconduct resulted in over 6,800 victims, 247 deaths, and cost over 345 million dollars in civil judgments or settlements. Of the reported incidents, excessive force led the complaints with nearly 24 percent of the cases, followed by sexual misconduct complaints at 9.3 percent. The next highest complaints were fraud or theft, accounting for just over 7 percent of cases and false arrest at nearly 7 percent.

Unsurprisingly, Queer victims of police brutality exist in great numbers, however it should be noted that any kind of victimization against Queer folks is grossly underreported. Buist and Stone (2014: 38) used the National Transgender Victimization Survey (NTVS), which includes responses from over 6,400 transgender and gender variant participants in the United States and surrounding territories, to highlight that "20% of respondents were denied equal treatment by police officers, 29% harassed or disrespected, and 6% reported physical assault by a police officer." Further, 46 percent of respondents reported some level of discomfort seeking the help of police officers (Buist & Stone 2014; Grant, Mottet, Tanis, Harrison, Herman, & Keislin 2011).

In addition to the NTVS, the National Coalition of Anti-Violence Programs (NCAVP) found that Queer people report being harassed and abused by the police at higher rates (at least 2–3 times higher) than others. What is perhaps most alarming is that there was a distinct increase in police misconduct towards Queer people who reported being victims of violence to the police from 31 percent in 2011 to 48 percent in 2012. Additionally, survivors of violence who reported their victimization to the police indicated that they were met with hostility nearly 30 percent of the time, an increase of nearly 20 percent from the previous report (NCAVP 2012).

However, as we mentioned at the onset of this section, how one might define or describe police abuse and in turn fear of law enforcement can be subjective. Fear of trans and/or homophobic reactions from the police are not uncommon. As we note throughout this examination, police encounters are often unsettling for the victims. For example, Buist and Stone (2014) note the now infamous interaction that Brandon Teena had with police officers when he went to report being raped by the men who would later murder him. In more detail, this is how the event took place: In Nebraska in the winter (December 24th or 25th) of 1993, Brandon Teena was beaten and raped by John Lotter and Tim Nissen after they had discovered that Brandon was born female. Brandon filed a report with law enforcement, but the subsequent interview conducted, primarily by Sheriff Charles Laux, revealed the ways in which trans victims are often further victimized by law enforcement. During the interview, which for all intents and purposes was an interrogation, Laux asked Brandon what he had in his underpants when Lotter and Nissen removed them, insinuating that Brandon used deception to appear male. Specifically, Laux asked Brandon if he used a sock to appear as if he had a penis, to which Brandon admitted. Later, when Brandon told Laux that the assailants did not touch Brandon sexually after finding out that he was biologically female, Laux responds that he doesn't believe that the men would not have touched Brandon in some way, going so far as to say that he did not believe that after pulling Brandon's pants down that Lotter and Nissen would not "stick his hand in you or his finger in you." Laux stated several times that he did not believe Brandon's story even though Brandon told Laux in great detail that he was beaten by Lotter and Nissen before being taken to their car and raped. Laux then asked Brandon how he was sitting in the car when Lotter and Nissen began to "poke" him.

Laux's entire tone and demeanor was nothing short of accusatory, again, repeating his disbelief that the event even took place while, stating that because Brandon was drunk he could not believe that his rapists would not have "played with" Brandon "a little bit." Further, Laux repeatedly asked Brandon how his legs were positioned in the car and if Lotter and/or Nissen penetrated him vaginally or anally. Laux accused Brandon of changing his statement about his position in the car and essentially accusing him of lying, stating that he could play the tape back in order to prove it to Brandon to which Brandon told him to do so. Court findings concluded that Brandon had not changed his account of the brutal attack. Laux then asked Brandon why he wanted to appear male and asked, "why do you run around with girls instead of guys beings [sic] you're a girl yourself? Why do you make girls think you're a guy?" Brandon responded that he was unsure as to why he did it and asked Laux what the relevance of those questions were, with Laux replying that he was attempting to ascertain all of the information pertaining to the night that Brandon was raped. Brandon later commented that he did not think that was important to the case and indicated that he had a "sexual identity crisis" but that he could not explain it.

What can be gleaned from this interaction is quite clearly an example of victim blaming and secondary victimization, but we can also see the Sheriff attempting to establish reasons why Lotter and Nissen would have beaten and raped Brandon – which relates to gay and trans panic defenses so often used in cases such as this, as Chapter 4 will highlight. Despite the fact that police obtained evidence that would support Brandon's attack and rape, that other officers believed Brandon, that Lotter and Nissen both admitted to assaulting Brandon, that numerous statements from Brandon and others corroborated the initial statement, and that Brandon was afraid that Lotter and Nissen would retaliate against him for going to the police, no immediate action was taken and Lotter and Nissen remained free. Approximately one week later, Lotter and Nissen murdered Brandon and two others (See *Brandon Estate of Brandon v. County of Richardson* 2001; Buist & Stone 2014; O'Hanlon 2001).

It is our cultural norms surrounding sexuality and gender presentation that make members of the Queer community vulnerable to abuse at the hands of law enforcement. As we have shown, members of the Queer community, especially transgender men and women, not only distrust the police and law enforcement in general, but fear the police as well. In countries around the world, Queer people are abused and victimized by officers who are sworn to uphold the law. In Kyrgyzstan, for example, where bisexual or gay men especially fear being "outed" to their communities, police are known to beat, extort, and rape them, knowing that their fear makes them easy targets (Human Rights Watch 2014). Despite the legality of consensual gay sex in Kyrgyzstan, the social stigma of homosexuality creates a space for extreme abuses against the Queer community and impunity for the offending officers. A Human Rights Watch report (2014) detailing the police brutality against gay men in Kyrgyzstan describes one victim's rape at the hands of police officers. The victim described being forced to the ground and that another officer "took his penis out and started forcing it in my mouth. One officer was holding me from behind and really hurting my arms. . . . Then he let my hands go, and took his pants off. They also said that they would also fuck me in the ass" (Human Rights Watch 2014: 39–40). Similar to the findings of the NCAVP (2012), the EU (European Union) LGBT equality survey, with over 90,000 respondents from EU member states and Croatia, found that in 43 percent of the most serious incidents of hate-motivated violence against Queer persons, half admitted that they did not think police would do anything about their victimization. Further, the report noted that one third of the participants indicated that they did not report hate crime victimization to the police because they feared a "transphobic or homophobic reaction from the police" (European Union Agency for Fundamental Rights 2014: 68).

Recently in Uganda where, as indicated in Chapter 2, all homosexual acts are considered illegal, gays and lesbians have reported being abused by police officers including "intrusive physical examinations" or being ignored or threatened by police. Gays and lesbians indicated that officers would refuse to investigate cases filed involving gay and lesbian victims or would charge them with a variety of behaviors that violate Ugandan criminal codes against homosexuality. They also noted that they experienced physical abuse from law enforcement and prison officials, as well as being coerced into making statements about themselves that were incriminating (BBC 2015).

Selective enforcement

Abuses of power in policing are manifested in more ways than just the physical. When addressing the selective enforcement that police officers implement through the use of discretionary tactics, we must note that these tactics often represent the personal beliefs and ideologies of the officer and/or department, larger political agendas, or antiquated discriminatory policy. Because of this and because of the overall fear that Queer people have of law enforcement officers and officials, the victimization of Queer people often goes unreported or is ignored, or they are revictimized by those who are supposed to be protecting them and their rights.

Gruenwald and Kelly (2014) reported that the NCVAP found that LGBT homicides in the United States have been increasing since 2007. In 2011, there were at least 30 anti-LGBT murders, which has been the highest reported number to date. These homicide victims were murdered based solely on their sexual orientation or, as noted by Gruenwald and Kelly (2014), their perceived sexual orientation. These acts of violence are oftentimes exceptionally brutal – in 30 percent of LGBT homicides, multiple weapons are used, and in 42 percent of homicides, there are multiple offenders. As with all hate-motivated crimes, the numbers are vastly underreported and therefore there is little to no way of knowing just how many homicides result from anti-Queer violence. What research has indicated is that because there is a constant disconnect between the Queer community and law enforcement and because members of the Queer community feel as though they are targeted by police, there is little reason to believe that all violence against the community is reported, or when reported, that those incidences are properly investigated.

For example, Greenberg (2011) indicates that trans women are less likely to seek help from police officers in cases of domestic violence and trans people of color are even less likely to report. The decision not to report is often for the same reasons that cisgender Black women are reluctant to report their victimization to police – because they already distrust the police and see no viable options in reporting an incident that will only further victimize themselves or their communities. Greenberg (2011: 232) goes on to note that transgender victims often express that they themselves are seen/treated as offenders simply because of their identity; "reading a trans woman as trans may cause the officer to doubt her story of abuse, especially if her abuser is perceived as a cisgender woman."

Additionally, transgender men and women often feel as though police officers use stop and frisk techniques not as a means of preventing crime but rather as a means to assess one's sex, or as Greenberg

(2011) calls them, "gender checks." Other problems associated with police responses to domestic violence and intimate partner abuse cases involving transgender individuals is the refusal of officers to assist because they assume that the victims are prostitutes (this speaks both to selective enforcement based on gender identity as well as selective enforcement based on personal ideology). Conversely, trans women have reported being disproportionately targeted based on what the community, as previously mentioned, has referred to as "walking while trans." This concept mirrors the racial disparities found with regards to selective enforcement focused on Black men when driving, or what Harris (1999) first coined, Driving While Black. This concept refers to pretextual traffic stops (deemed legal by the Supreme Court) of Black men in particular using the traffic stop as a means to produce reasonable suspicion and probable cause in order to search the men and their vehicles hoping to ascertain and obtain illegal drugs. Returning to the concept of walking while trans, a study conducted by the Department of Justice on the New Orleans Police Department found that "members of the LGBT community complained that NOPD officers subject them to unjustified arrests for prostitution, targeting bars frequented by the community and sometimes fabricating evidence of solicitation for compensation" (Greenberg 2011: 231). Interestingly enough, in the previously cited Cato Institute report from 2010, the state with the highest misconduct rate was Louisiana (it should be noted that while they lead in misconduct rate, they are not the leaders in the number of officers involved in each incident).

In Australia, Dwyer's (2011) research indicated that police interaction with LGBT youth impacted the way police treated them and how the police chose to use discretion. Much like in the United States, Australian youth felt harassed and victimized and in turn were reluctant to report their victimizations to law enforcement. Indeed, if there is an increase in the negative interactions between young LGBT people, this will in turn impact their belief in police legitimacy (Dwyer 2011). Dwyer also indicated that police tried to assess sexual orientation based on gender constructions of masculinities and femininities and gender performance, i.e. feminine boys were harassed based on their outward appearance, or "how the body can be performed in ways that visibly enact queerness and in turn is constituted as a body to be watched and regulated by police" (Dwyer 2011: 216).

In the United States, a 2014 report from the Office of Juvenile Justice and Delinquency investigated "LGBTQ Youth in the Juvenile Justice System" (in this case the "Q" stood for "questioning" rather than "Queer"). Much of this report will be detailed in Chapter 5, but until then, it should be noted that similar to the Australian-based study on young people, in the United States, LGBTQ juveniles are more likely to be stopped by police, which leads to a disproportionate representation of LGBT youth in the juvenile system. What is important to keep in mind is that with an increased number of LGBTQ-identified young people on the streets, it is not unlikely that they will have contact with the police. But what is of major importance here is to remember that once in the criminal legal system there is an increased likelihood that one will remain trapped in the criminal legal system. For instance, research has found that disproportionate minority contact with police leads to an overrepresentation of young minorities in courtrooms and correctional facilities.

Historically, this research has focused on the disproportionate contact that people, primarily young people of color, have with police, but research has also indicated that the media often influences the public perception of crime and criminals and the perception of people of color as offenders. Images of offenders as young, minority, poor, and from urban settings (Reiman & Leighton 2012; see Russell 1998) can certainly affect the ways in which police officers choose to selectively enforce law-breaking behavior even if those behaviors are nonviolent, such as hanging out in a local park or on a street corner. This influence should be considered when we examine the ways in which young people who identify or are labeled as Queer are treated by law enforcement and understand that these youth are also being contacted by police officers in disproportionate numbers. This contact serves no greater good, but instead serves to further marginalize minority populations in the United States and abroad. Research has shown that while Queer youth make up no more than 7 percent of the US population, they currently represent up to 15 percent of the population within our juvenile justice system (Hunt & Moodie-Mills

2012; OJJDP 2014). Further, as indicated earlier, many of these young people are forced out of their homes and into the streets because of their sexual orientation and/or gender identity, and tend to commit survival crimes rather than predatory violence. Finally, the impact of intersectionality is quite real for these young people, as over 60 percent of these Queer youth are Black or Latino (Hunt & Moodie-Mills 2012).

In the following section, we turn our attention to the differential treatment that Queer law enforcement officers experience on the job. Several studies will be highlighted that do show some improvement in the working conditions for Queer officers in police departments around the world. However, officers still report feeling marginalized and harassed at work and many of them fear being out or outed on the job. First, we must discuss the policing structure and culture that is in place and may influence the negative ways in which Queer officers are treated.

Queer and blue

In order to address the experiences of officers who identify as lesbian, gay, bisexual, transgender, or queer, we must first discuss the policing subculture. Historically, policing has been a male-dominated field that values masculine traits while devaluing traits that are commonly attributed to women. Therefore, physical aggression is viewed as an essential component of police work instead of or above verbal communication; or an officer will value communication skills but will argue that at some point the talking has to end and the fight has to begin – therefore physical strength is required. Mind you, there is rarely any discussion of the value of the tools that all officers have at their disposal regardless of their sex (Corsianos 2009; Wells & Alt 2005). Even today, women make up less than 20 percent of law enforcement officials. Regardless of a new generation of police officers that may not identify gender stereotypes on the job as much as before, women are still seen as the outsiders within a male profession. Women officers who present in a more masculine way on the job often comment that this works as more of a benefit than detriment to them (Corsianos 2009; Miller, Forest, & Jurik 2003). In fact, Miller et al. (2003) noted that lesbians who are out on the job feel as though because this is almost expected, they are not as marginalized as gay men are. However, in total, research has indicated that gay and lesbian officers experience a heightened sense of marginalization and harassment compared to other minority groups on the job (Colvin 2009; Moran 2007; see also Bernstein & Kostelac 2002; Buhrke 1996; Burke 1994; Miller et al. 2003).

Focusing on the value placed on masculinity and the vast numbers of men working in policing is important because they both serve to explain the heteronormative culture that is pervasive in male-dominated jobs, or more specifically, the influence of compulsory heterosexuality within the policing occupation (Miller et al. 2003). Therefore, identifying as anything other than straight can prove detrimental, perhaps especially to gay male officers. Some of the findings in Miller et al. (2003) reveal that gay and lesbian officers felt as though they were constantly scrutinized, excluded by their heterosexual colleagues, and were victims of a variety of antigay behaviors. Other concerns voiced were fear that if officers were out on the job, their fellow officers would fail to back them up on duty calls, and that they feared being viewed as distrustful if others found out they were gay, as well as experiencing a lack of camaraderie on the job (Miller et al. 2003). Since officers distrust the public and put an immense amount of trust in their fellow officers, being shunned by your colleagues can have potentially dangerous, even life-threatening results. While some have found support for being out on the job (see Colvin 2009; Jones 2015), there must be consideration for officers who are not out to their families or friends, let alone at work. Just as some officers interviewed by Colvin (2009) and Miller et al. (2003) have indicated that being out can benefit them (allow them to be open about their relationship status, gain respect of other officers, speak freely about their personal lives, etc.) this can also have a backlash effect, as noted earlier, with regards to overt or covert harassment and lack of support on the job, including going on calls and requiring back-up that may never arrive.

Other qualitative studies have brought attention to the victimization, harassment, and marginalization of gay and lesbian officers. For instance, in her book, *A Matter of Trust*, Buhrke (1996) presents narrative interviews with over 40 men and women, representing over

30 different departments in law enforcement, detailing their personal experiences on the job. Buhrke begins the introduction of her research by revealing her personal experiences as a police officer and being viewed as a "traitor" amongst the Queer community.

Officers all too often are not accepted by their police community because they are gay and lesbian, and because they are cops, they are rejected by the lesbian and gay community.

Buhrke 1996: 2

Research indicates that gay and lesbian officers remain committed to policing as a profession and often times are just as embedded in the organizational environment of the job as any other officer (e.g. Burke 1994; Corsianos 2009; Miller et al. 2003). This level of commitment to the profession and dedication to the work is exemplified by the Queer officers who stay on the job despite facing harassment and stereotypes that are shrouded in the patriarchal masculinist organization of policing itself. An extreme example of this is highlighted in a study by Buist (2011), in which a lesbian officer commented that while on the job, she had experienced varying levels of harassment including being stalked by a coworker, another coworker identifying her as lesbian although she wasn't out, and experiencing having investigations opened against her and her partner, all of which ultimately led to her leaving law enforcement. Despite the torment, she later returned to the academy and policing because of her dedication and love of the job, regardless of the hate she had experienced. Indeed, many of the lesbian officers who discussed their personal histories on the job noted that although they experienced more incidents of harassment because of their sexual orientation, they remained in law enforcement because they loved the work. Still, they admitted that as women and as lesbians they felt as though they had to work much harder than anyone else to prove that they belonged (Buist 2011). As indicated in previous studies (see Miller et al. 2003) Corsianos (2009: 105) notes that lesbians "like other officers . . . wanted to be recognized for their traditional policing goals."

As mentioned previously, one of the major issues that will no doubt continue to impact Queer officers' decisions to be on the job, let alone out on the job, may be attributed to the ideology of fellow officers as well as their superiors, up to and including the head of their respective agencies. Not to mention the political climate and influence both at the federal and state levels. While there has been a federal ban on discrimination that is based on sexual orientation, this does not mean that every state follows the same policy. In the United States today, not all states consider sexual orientation or gender orientation to be protected classes and this certainly may be a contributing factor as to why some officers choose to stay in the closet rather than disclosing their sexual and/or gender orientation. Many departments across the country and abroad have begun to implement new training strategies with the intention of recruiting officers with more diverse backgrounds as well as updating their codes of conduct to reflect a more diverse workforce and implementing and requiring new training techniques for officers who come into contact with Queer communities and individuals. The question, however, remains: Do these approaches work? Also, how can the policing style used by a department influence the way in which training is implemented and instituted?

Policing ştyle and training

In a recent study conducted in England and Wales, Jones (2015) surveyed 836 police officers to assess if a move to diversify policing was successful. Jones highlighted many of the findings from Burke's (1994) work that addressed the negative experiences faced by LGB people, which included feeling hostility and aggression from police, that their concerns and protection were ignored by police officers, and that LGB officers themselves felt as though they were viewed as deviant because of their sexual orientation. Jones's (2015) latest report concentrates on the attempt to bring law enforcement more up-to-date regarding not only the public's image of the police departments but the ways in which the officers do their jobs and relate and/or accept each other. Specifically, the departments in England and Wales were focused on improving their department in order to

...fracture the dominance of white, heterosexual men in policing and resultant informal working practices, through active
recruitment of officers from a broad spectrum of cultural and
demographic backgrounds.

(Jones 2015: 3)

The findings of Jones's (2015) survey were promising, noting that
there was positive change in the departments in England and Wales.
Indeed, Jones (2015: 5) indicated that over 70 percent of survey
respondents indicated that their departments "do enough for LGB
cops," that they are "satisfied or very satisfied" as police officers in
their departments and over 80 percent of respondents noted that they
had not encountered prejudice on the job because they identified
as LGBTQ. Much of these positive results may be attributed to the
change in legislation in England and Wales, as well as the decision
of the police there to implement their own changes to their police
code of conduct to include "respect and courtesy, honesty, and integ-
rity, personal autonomy, lawfulness and professional equity" (2015:
6). Although these findings are positive to say the least, officers still
reported feelings of distress and discrimination, but at a lower percentage than before the changes were implemented.

Additionally, Jones (2015) highlights a salient point regarding
sexuality and sexual orientation. He notes that we must appreciate
that sexual orientation or identity is dynamic and that to attempt to
understand sexuality is also to recognize the intricacies that accom-
pany sexual as well as gender identities. As indicated in Chapter 1, we
must be cognizant and aware that sexuality for some may be considered a construction that is influenced by a litany of factors and tied
into the influence of the patriarchal society in which we live. Further,
these ideas that we develop based on gender role expectations are
often manifested through imitation and reproduction of those expectations of masculinity and femininity (Butler 1990; West & Zimmerman 1987). Instead of essentialist and absolutist thinking regarding
sexual orientation and/or gender identity, we should be able to recognize the continuum of sexuality that exists or may exist for some.
Conversely, the criminal legal system, when functioning properly,
identifies behavior based on codified laws that are often interpreted

literally as opposed to focusing on the myriad interpretations that may exist. Here, we have police officers who are tasked with being the frontline guardians of law enforcement and therefore they may be even less apt to adopt an understanding of the possibility of fluidity as applied to identity. Officers often rely heavily upon their use of discretion, at times to the detriment of citizens and officers alike (see selective enforcement). Therefore, officers continue to classify individuals based on what they *know*, because the unknown is what they most fear.

The style of policing that is promoted and implemented within the policing occupation will have a significant impact on the effectiveness of diversity training among officers. The move from the professional era of policing into a more problem-oriented era and now into community-oriented policing may indeed not only serve to foster tolerance, understanding, and acceptance of Queer officers and citizens, but it may also begin to attract different kinds of people to the law enforcement profession in general. Keep in mind that more traditional forms of policing – such as the problem-oriented and broken-windows styles, along with and perhaps especially zero-tolerance or quality-of-life policing – have proven to promote distrust of citizens towards officers. For example, when William Bratton instituted zero-tolerance policing in the NYPD, he argued that the method of policing would help to clean up the streets and subway stations of the homeless population. Essentially, this style of policing enforces a variety of laws against loitering and vagrancy. When describing subway stations throughout the city he commented:

> Every platform seemed to have a cardboard city where the homeless had taken up residence. This was a city that had stopped caring about itself. There was a sense of permissive society allowing certain things that would not have been permitted years ago.
>
> (Bratton 1998: 34)

While Bratton had argued that quality-of-life policing is similar to problem-oriented and community-oriented policing, this argument is problematic especially since upon instituting zero-tolerance policing, citizen complaint reports of police brutality increased by 75 percent and Amnesty International found a 60 percent increase in citizen complaints in the early to mid-1990s (Green 1999). More recently, the NYPD has been in the center of debate regarding stop and frisk laws that unduly impact people of color. Any style of policing, such as zero-tolerance law enforcement, has a tendency to clean the streets at the detriment of minority populations, often poor, homeless, people of color. But at the same time, we must keep in mind that our youth population is also targeted and affected by the enforcement of these laws, and certainly our Queer youth as they experience higher rates of homelessness.

Instead of using styles of policing that are reactionary, community policing involves the concerns of the residents and business owners promoting what Alpert, Durham, and Stroshine (2006: 97) identify as the open-systems theory: A design that is "flexible, adaptive, and organic." While Alpert et al. argue that this particular approach to community policing would fall within the professional model, there is certainly room for debate here as professional styles of policing are more reactionary than proactive, which is one of the central tenets of community-oriented policing strategies. Greene (2004) suggests that law enforcement officers should view the public as "clients," which in essence brings attention to the importance of knowing the community that the officers patrol; therefore, interaction with the community members will better allow them to assess the needs of that community. Several different scholars have indicated that the structure of policing in and of itself, the paramilitaristic hierarchical model that values masculinity and aggression, prevents the successful implementation of community-policing styles. However, Greenberg (1999) asserts that it is not the structure that should be blamed, but instead the people working within the structure that should be held accountable, namely those in supervisory roles, for the failure to successfully implement community policing and establish positive relationships with the members of the community. This is certainly an interesting observation, however, if the organization itself was restructured in a way that did not support individuals' prejudiced beliefs or encourage those beliefs, a message would be sent that intolerance is unacceptable – this was evidenced in the aforementioned study by Jones (2015) that found a dramatic change in the experiences of Queer officers once new and more inclusive training had been implemented.

The Ontario Association of Chiefs of Police issued a report, "Best Practices in Policing and LGBTQ Communities in Ontario," in 2013, which was the first of its kind to be published in Canada (Kirkup 2013). The report addressed past practices that promoted tensions between the police and the LGBTQ community throughout Toronto and detailed the importance of implementing policing strategies that were inclusive of all members of the communities they policed, noting that "police services should reflect the communities they serve" (Kirkup 2013: 9). The report also highlighted the Canadian Association of Chiefs of Police adoption of Resolution 2 in 2004 that noted the importance of policing free of bias, and that rather focused on "fairness, dignity, and ethics" (2013: 6). This mirrors the code of conduct that police in England and Wales adopted (Jones 2015) that connotes the importance of respect and honesty among others (see above). Another important aspect in how training should reflect the changing face of communities and policing itself is in recognizing the importance of respecting "safe spaces" of Queer members. Moran (2007: 418) points out "safe spaces are often created in response to homophobic violence exploring personal, community, commercial and institutional responses to threatened and actual violence." Police therefore, must understand that these locations are seen not only as safe spaces for Queer folks, but sacred places as well; places where individuals who feel marginalized in many if not all of the social settings they reside in can feel accepted and protected. Police officers who have no knowledge of the prejudices that Queer people have experienced are less likely to understand just how important these places are and how valued they are by the community of people that they serve.

In relation to the importance of safe spaces, it is also important to understand that the population in a particular area will influence the knowledge of the community itself. If there is not a known presence of Queer folks in a particular area, these areas may in fact be the locations where police need the most training and awareness regarding issues that impact people who are unlike themselves. As for police officers who are Queer, one could surmise that the smaller the department, the less likely an officer will feel safe being out or coming out on the job. Either way, we continue to see prejudiced attitudes towards Queer officers regardless of the size of the police department. We also must understand that hate and prejudice are not always known on the job, but rather suspected. This again speaks to personal politics and ideology that departments can do little about until those prejudices manifest themselves. For example, Lyons, DeValve, and Garner (2008: 110) found that of the 747 police chiefs in Texas they surveyed, nearly 50 percent of them reported that they had "trouble working with a gay man," while over 60 percent reported that "homosexuality constitutes a 'moral turpitude,'" and 56 percent indicated that being gay was a "perversion." Additionally, 58 percent of their participants "believed that lesbians and gay men have a choice in their desires."

Law enforcement is facing a backlash of their own – especially with the use of social media, every misstep and poor decision is broadcast on the nightly news and across Twitter feeds throughout the world. But, unlike most professions, when police officers make poor decisions, people can die. When those decisions are couched within prejudice and hatred, there is little that policing style, training, or even legislation can do to protect those who are the victims of police violence or victims of the discrimination that prevents officers from protecting and serving the public regardless of sexual orientation, gender orientation, or the color of one's skin, among so many other intersecting oppressions.

Returning to the discussion of community policing, this conversation is relevant, especially in the face of what appears to be increased (or perhaps the increased knowledge of) brutality and selective enforcement of minority citizens. As noted, theoretically speaking, community-oriented policing focuses on proactive interpersonal connections and interactions between officers and the public. There are problems associated with this as most police departments would espouse that they utilize community-oriented practices; however, this is rarely the case. Again, if the structure of policing or law enforcement in general is couched within paramilitaristic, patriarchal, hypermasculine ideals, these strategies will never result in the relational approach that is community-oriented policing. Instead, the institution will continue to operate by utilizing aggressive tactics that in turn, as shown, result in increased civilian complaints and distrust between civilians and officers, between officers and civilians, and in the case of Queer officers, between officers and officers.

If community-oriented policing is to be effective, then it needs to be implemented correctly and completely – no more half measures that are implemented perhaps because federal funding is granted to departments who claim some degree of community policing. The Bureau of Justice Statistics (BJS) reports that 83 percent of officers in the United States work in departments that claim to use community police officers (Hickman & Reaves 2006). Therefore, the odds are that departments that report having community policing officers and promote community policing tactics are likely to be implementing selective enforcement and disproportionate profiling strategies that impact Queer communities, communities of color, and poor communities. Instead of simply stating that community policing is being utilized, there needs to be an effort to incorporate the tenets of community-oriented policing beyond the surface-level work of checking in with community leaders and/or giving officers some modicum of responsibility in decision making on patrol.

So how does law enforcement properly and successfully implement community-oriented policing? First, we would suggest that departments use successful models to guide them in changing their own policy and approaches to policing. Next, we would suggest supervisory positions within the department that monitor the successful implementation of community-oriented policing strategies and working groups of officers who are assigned community roles, much like a community liaison within the police department. In general, we would also recommend a move away from the traditional, aggressive style of policing that has done little to serve communities, states, and nations. This would require a complete change in the structure of the institution of policing and would not come without substantial backlash. We understand that this is not likely to occur, but if recruitment strategies were changed, and codes of conduct updated and enforced and violation of such codes were punished, we may see a more inclusive law enforcement component of the criminal legal system. Research, although scant, has indicated that some positive changes can develop. Still, Queer officers remain marginalized within their departments. Their best defense is most likely changing legislation that protects against discrimination based on sexual and/or gender orientation, but that legislation has yet to be implemented in all 50 states in the United States. Further, while legislation will allow for protections in the eyes of the law, this does not mean that it will guarantee equal treatment for Queer officers.

Recommended viewing

Boys Don't Cry, 1999 [Film] Directed by Kimberly Peirce. USA: Fox Searchlight.
The Brandon Teena Story, 1998 [Film] Directed by Susan Muska & Gréta Olafsdóttir. USA: Zeitgeist Films.

References

Alpert, G.P., Durham, R.G., & Stroshine, M.S. 2006. *Policing: Continuity and change.* Long Grove, IL: Waveland Press.

BBC. 2015. *Ugandan gay people "abused by police."* BBC News, February 27. Accessed from http://www.bbc.com/news/world-africa-31658311.

Becker, H. 1963. *Outsiders.* New York, NY: The Free Press.

Bernstein, M. & Kostelac, C. 2002. *Lavender and blue: Attitudes about homosexuality and behavior toward lesbian and gay men among police officers. Journal of Contemporary Criminal Justice, 18,* (3): 302–328.

Brandon Estate of Brandon v. County of Richardson. 2001. Accessed from http://caselaw.findlaw.com/ne-supreme-court/1275811.html.

Bratton, W.J. 1998. *Crime is down in New York City: Blame the police.* In Norman Dennis (ed.), *Zero tolerance: Policing a free society* (pp. 29–42). London, UK: IEA.

Buhrke, R. 1996. *A matter of justice: Lesbians and gay men in law enforcement.* New York, NY: Routledge.

Buist, C. 2011. *"Don't let the job change you; you change the job": The lived experiences of women in policing.* Dissertations. Paper 335. http://scholarworks.wmich.edu/dissertations/355.

Buist, C.L. & Stone, C. 2014. *Transgender victims and offenders: Failures of the United States criminal justice system and the necessity of queer criminology. Critical Criminology, 22,* (1): 35–47.

Burke, M. 1994. *Homosexuality as deviance: The case of the gay police officer. British Journal of Criminology, 34* (2): 192–203.

Butler, J. 1990. *Gender Trouble.* New York, NY: Routledge.

Cao, L. 2003. *Curbing police brutality: What works? A reanalysis of citizen complaints at the organizational level.* Washington, DC: United States Department of Justice: National Criminal Justice Reference Service.

Collins, P. 2000. *Black feminist thought: Knowledge, consciousness, and the politics of empowerment*. New York, NY: Routledge.

Colvin, R. 2009. *Shared perceptions among lesbian and gay police officers: Barriers and opportunities in the law enforcement work environment. Police Quarterly, 12*, (1): 86–101.

Colvin, R. 2012. *Gay and lesbian cops: Diversity and effective policing*. Boulder, CO: Reinner.

Corsianos, M. 2009. *Policing and gendered justice: Examining the possibilities*. Toronto, Canada: University of Toronto Press.

Crenshaw, K. 1989. *Mapping the margins: Intersectionality, identity politics, and violence against women of color. Stanford Law Review, 43*: 1240–1299.

Dwyer, A. 2011. *"It's not like we're going to jump them": How transgressing heteronormativity shapes police interactions with LGBT young people. Youth Justice, 11*, (3): 203–220.

European Union Agency for Fundamental Rights. 2014. *EU LGBT survey: European Union lesbian, gay, bisexual and transgender survey*. Luxembourg: Publications Office of the European Union.

Foucault, M. 1980. *Power/knowledge: Selected interviews and other writings*. New York, NY: Pantheon Press.

Garza, A. 2014. *A herstory of the #blacklivesmatter movement by Alicia Garza. The Feminist Wire*, October 7. Accessed from http://thefeministwire. com/2014/10/blacklivesmatter-2/.

Grant, J., Mottet, L., Tanis, J., Harrison, J., Herman, J.L., & Keislin, M. 2011. *Injustice at every turn: A report of the national transgender discrimination survey*. Washington, DC: National Center for Transgender Equality & National Gay and Lesbian Task Force.

Green, J. 1999. *Zero tolerance: A case study of police policies and practices in New York City. Crime and Delinquency, 45*, (2): 171–187.

Greenberg, K. 2011. *Still hidden in the closet: Trans women and domestic violence. Berkeley Journal of Gender, Law & Justice*: 198–251.

Greenberg, S. 1999. *Is it time to change law enforcement's paramilitary structure?* In Sewell, J.D. & Egger, S.A. (eds.), *Controversial issues in policing* (pp. 139–153). Brockleigh, NJ: Allyn and Bacon.

Greene, J.R. 2004. *Community policing and police organization*. In Skogan, W.G. (ed.), *Community policing: Can it work?* (pp. 30–54). Belmont, CA: Thomson Wadsworth.

Gruenwald, J. & Kelly, K. 2014. *Exploring anti-LGBT homicide by mode of victim selection. Criminal Justice and Behavior, 41*, (9): 1130–1152.

Harris, D. 1999. *The stories, the statistic, and the law: Why "driving while black" matters. Minnesota Law Review, 84*: 265–326.

Hickman, M.J. & Reaves, B.A. 2006. *Local police departments, 2003*. Washington, DC: Bureau of Justice Statistics.

Human Rights Watch. 2014. *"They said we deserved this": Police violence against gay and bisexual men in Kyrgyzstan.* United States of America: Human Rights Watch.

Hunt, J. & Moodie-Mills, A. 2012. *The unfair criminalization of gay and transgender youth: An overview of the experiences of LGBT youth in juvenile justice system.* Washington, DC: Center for American Progress.

Jones, M. 2015. *Who forgot lesbian, gay, and bisexual police officers? Findings from a national survey. Policing, 9*, (1): 1–12.

Kirkup, K. 2013. *Best practices in policing and LGBTQ communities in Ontario.* Ontario, Canada: Ontario Association of Chiefs of Police.

Lee, J. 2014. *Here's the data that shows cops kill black people at a higher rate than white people. Mother Jones,* September 10. Accessed from http://www. motherjones.com/politics/2014/08/police-shootings-ferguson-race-data.

Lyons Jr., P.M., DeValve, M.J., & Garner, R.L. 2008. *Texas police chiefs' attitudes toward gay and lesbian police officers. Police Quarterly, 11*, (1): 102–117.

Miller, S.L., Forest, K.B., & Jurik, N.C. 2003. *Diversity in blue: Lesbian and gay police officers in a masculine occupation. Men and Masculinities, 5*, (4): 355–385.

Mogul, J.L., Ritchie, A., & Whitlock, K. 2011. *Queer (in)justice: The criminalization of LGBT people in the United States.* Boston, MA: Beacon Press.

Moran, L.J. 2007. *"Invisible minorities": Challenging community and neighbourhood models of policing. Criminology & Criminal Justice, 7*, (4): 417–441.

National Coalition of Anti-Violence Programs. 2012. *Lesbian, gay, bisexual, transgender, queer and HIV-affected hate violence in 2012.* New York, NY: National Coalition of Anti-Violence Programs.

Office of Juvenile Justice and Delinquency Prevention. 2014. *LGBTQ Youth in the Juvenile Justice System.* Washington, DC: N/A.

O'Hanlon, K. 2001. *Brandon Teena's mother sues sheriff. ABC News,* January 13. Accessed from http://abcnews.go.com/US/story?id=94389.

Reiman, J. & Leighton, P. 2012. *The rich get richer and the poor get prison: Ideology, class, and criminal justice.* Boston, MA: Pearson.

Russell, K. 1998. *The color of crime: Racial hoaxes, white fear, black protectionism, police harassments, and other microaggressions.* New York, NY: New York University Press.

Wells, S.K. & Alt, B.L. 2005. *Police women: Life with the badge.* Westport, CT: Praeger.

West, C. & Zimmerman, D.H. 1987. *Doing gender. Gender & Society 1*, (2): 125–151.

4

QUEER CRIMINOLOGY AND LEGAL SYSTEMS

While Chapter 3 focused on Queer experiences with or as law enforcement officers, here we turn our attention to what happens in courtrooms around the globe. Not only will we explore the ways that Queer rights have been battled out in the courts and how laws and criminal trials affect Queer offenders and victims, but we will also identify how non-Queer offenders have come to use systems of homophobia and heteronormativity to their advantage. Additionally, we will explore how laws can (or cannot) be used to address crimes committed against the Queer community.

The battle for queer rights

As delineated in Chapter 2, queerness in and of itself continues to be criminalized throughout the world, so it is not surprising that Queer people are denied equal treatment in nearly every social institution including employment, marriage, and education, among others. The denial of these rights affects all Queer citizens, including those entrenched in the criminal legal system and the attainment or denial of those rights are oft determined by judges in a court of law.

According to a report submitted to the International Lesbian Gay Bisexual Trans and Intersex Association (Itaborahy & Zhu 2014), employment discrimination based on sexual orientation is prohibited in only 61 countries. Unfortunately, only some states in the United States have banned such discrimination. This means that Queer people working within the criminal legal system must constantly fear the loss of their livelihood, which is exactly what happened to Crystal Moore, the openly lesbian police chief of Latta, South Carolina. Moore was fired from her position by Mayor Earl Bullard, a man who has made no secret of his antigay beliefs (Collins 2014). Despite the fact that South Carolina allows for discrimination based on sexual orientation, the citizens of Latta rallied behind Moore – not only did Moore get reinstated, but Bullard was stripped of most of his power by a majority vote in an ad-hoc election. While Moore's case resulted in a victory of sorts, it left her with $20,000 in legal bills and does not change the fact that Bullard was completely within his rights to fire her based on her sexuality.

Gay couples can marry in some parts or all of 11 countries and can join in some sort of civil union in 11 others – altogether that is less than 12 percent of the countries in the world (Itaborahy & Zhu 2014). The Netherlands became the first country to legalize gay marriage as recently as 2000, followed three years later by Belgium (Pew Research Center 2013). Though the wave of gay marriage legislation around the world has been seen as a victory for gay rights, the increasing recognition of gay marriage is not without negative consequence, as there has been notable backlash. Immediately before France legalized gay marriage in 2013, more than 45,000 citizens rallied against the proposed legislation – just one of dozens of demonstrations that required the presence of police suited in riot gear (Erlanger & Sayare 2013). The legislation was followed by a startling uptick in anti-LGBTQ violence, with the group *SOS Homophobie* reporting a 78 percent increase in homophobic incidents (3,500 in total) from the year prior (Potts 2014).

In the United States, where all states now have legal gay marriage, there has also been considerable backlash. Some nonviolent examples of this backlash were shared in Chapter 2, but lesbian, gay and bisexual citizens who have married legally have also faced some blatantly violent physical repercussions. For example, only nine days after marrying her female partner and being featured on local television stations as a result, a 28-year-old, Michigan woman was beaten unconscious by a group of men who yelled "Hey bitch, aren't you that faggot from the news?" (Ferrigno 2014) The victim's marriage was one of around 300 that occurred the day after a district court judge ruled the state's ban on gay marriage was unconstitutional – just 24 hours later, a stay prevented any more marriages from occurring and the state's ban had been upheld until the Supreme Court ruled gay marriage legal in June 2015. Despite the crime clearly being related to the victim's sexual orientation, Michigan's hate crime law would not apply even if her assailants were caught, as it does not include sexual orientation as a protected status.

Before even reaching the age of employability or being able to (possibly) marry, Queer youth face rampant discrimination and violence in school (Kosciw, Greytak, Palmer, & Beosen 2014; Snapp, Heonig, Fields, & Russell 2014). According to the 2013 school climate survey, conducted by the Gay Lesbian & Straight Education Network (GLSEN), over half of LGBT students do not feel safe at school because of their sexual orientation and 38.7 percent do not feel safe as a result of their gender expression (Kosciw et al. 2014). This feeling of unease is perpetuated by negative comments and language regarding sexual and gender orientation, over half of which students report hearing from school faculty and staff, and is validated by experiences of physical and violent attacks. Consequently, Queer students who experience victimization miss more school, have lower GPAs, experience greater rates of depression, report low levels of self-esteem, and are less likely to pursue college than their peers who do not experience victimization. Further, while more current anti-bullying laws are in place, these do little to protect the victim as all reporting responsibilities fall on the child; in truth, these laws are in place more to protect the school than the victim. All of these experiences contribute to the unique pathways that impact Queer youth, and in turn result in disproportionate interactions with police, courts, and eventually corrections within the criminal legal system.

In addition to being at greater risk of victimization, Queer youth may also be pegged as "offenders" more often than non-Queer youth and, consequently, may be disproportionately funneled into the school-to-prison pipeline (Himmelstein & Bruckner 2011; Kosciw et al. 2014; Snapp et al. 2014). Himmelstein and Bruckner (2011) found that Queer youth, especially nonheterosexual females, were more likely than their heterosexual peers to face a variety of sanctions including expulsion, arrest, detainment, and conviction. Another study by Snapp et al. (2014) contextualize these findings with examples of Queer youth being disproportionately punished for an array of behaviors including public displays of affection (both actual and rumored), violating school dress code, defending themselves from bullies, and truancy (which may of course be related to the aforementioned victimization). A brief released by the Gay-Straight Alliance Network (Burdge, Licona, & Hyemingway 2014) reveals that LGBT youth of color perceive themselves to be under greater surveillance by school police officers, faculty, and other school officials than their non-Queer peers, a finding not inconsistent with what is already known about racial disparity in the school-to-prison pipeline. Once again, the significance of intersectionality is revealed.

While on the surface, one's rights to nondiscriminatory employment, marriage, and safe schools seem to be civil issues, they are deeply entwined within the criminal legal system. As long as there are no employment protections for sexual or gender minorities, Queer criminal legal practitioners will not have job security. As long as gay marriage continues to divide people around the world, law enforcement will be left with the responsibility of policing protest and attending to the victims of backlash. As long as Queer youth are disproportionately funneled into the school-to-prison pipeline, the criminal legal system has no hope of fixing the vicious cycle of mass incarceration. Thus, the advancement of Queer rights in the civil arena should be of central concern to criminal legal practitioners and criminologists, but it cannot be left in their hands alone to protect the Queer community or to forge the fight for sexual and gender equality.

The advancement of Queer rights is largely due to and dependent upon LGBTI groups around the globe, and these organizations receive a majority of their financial support from the global North, particularly from grantmakers in the United States and Western Europe (Espinoza 2007). A 2005 study by Funders for Lesbian and Gay Issues (Espinoza 2007) found that 93 percent of grant dollars funding organizations in the global South, East, and North originated in the global North. Most of those grant dollars stayed in the global North, and nearly half of all of the grants totaled less than $10,000 USD. The 205 Queer organizations surveyed received a total of 328 grants, totaling almost $10.5 million dollars, 68 percent of which went to just 20 organizations. Many of these organizations operate with few or no paid employees and most, especially outside of the global North, are less than ten years old. Some of them remain unregistered out of fear of repercussions or because the governments under which they operate have placed barriers upon them. These figures highlight the challenges faced by organizations that are working to improve the lives of Queer citizens, especially as private funders increasingly pull away from Queer issues and human rights funders shift their focus to security and terrorism (Espinoza 2007). Moreover, it should be noted that the largest and most influential Queer rights groups (e.g. Human Rights Campaign) focus much of their effort on issues most relevant to those who run them (i.e. middle-class, gay, white men). For instance, some argue that a primary focus on marriage equality is short-sided when Black trans women are being murdered at an alarming rate. While great strides have been made, it is not safe to say that a quick, clear, or linear path to equality for *all* has been forged.

Domestic and international communities are truly at a crossroads in terms of gay rights. More than ever before, identity politics are playing out around the world and the results of that battle remain to be seen. Legal scholars continue to debate the role that legal decisions regarding civil rights will have for the overall advancement of Queer equality (Keck 2009). As illuminated here and in Chapter 2, there is no doubt that backlash does occur in the immediate wake of pro-LGBTQ legal decisions, but there is not a consensus about whether this backlash is simply an inevitable hiccup that will eventually dissipate, or if it can have a long-term and devastating effect on the overall path to equality. Some have argued that the magnitude of this backlash has been overstated. In his analysis of same-sex marriage decisions (and the resulting backlash) in the United States between 1993 and 2008, Keck (2009: 182) concludes that "the backlash narrative captures several important features of the recent history of LGBT rights litigation, but it does not support the sweeping and one-sided conclusions that have often been drawn from it." Whichever is truly the case, there is no denying that Queer people continue to take two steps forward and then find themselves forced to take one step back in regards to their equal rights. Moreover, the backlash that clearly exists, no matter how temporary, does affect social attitudes and therefore has an immediate effect on the treatment of Queer people in social institutions, including as employees, jurors, defendants, and victims in a court of law.

Queer experiences in the courtroom

Whether as lawyers, judges, jurors, defendants, civil litigants, or victims, Queer people that find themselves in a court of law face widespread homophobia and discrimination (Brower 2011; Cramer 2002; Farr 2000; Lee 2013; Meidinger 2012; Mogul 2005; Mogul, Ritchie, & Whitlock 2011; Shay 2014; Shortnacy 2001). The first large-scale exploration into courtroom bias regarding sexual orientation was conducted by the *Sexual Orientation Fairness Subcommittee* (SOFS 2001) of the *Access and Fairness Advisory Committee* of the Judicial Council in California in 1998 and 1999. The subcommittee used information garnered from five focus groups to develop a survey instrument that they distributed to gay and lesbian court users (n=1,225) and employees of all sexual orientations (n=1,525). Though most of the court users felt that they were treated the same as their heterosexual counterparts, over half (56%) reported experiencing or seeing negative comments or actions against gays and lesbians. Most of those negative experiences were reportedly felt when sexual orientation became an issue in relation to the case and most of the negative comments or actions were made by lawyers or court employees, not other court users. Of the court employees, 20 percent reported hearing derogatory comments or jokes about gays or lesbians, most often made by lawyers and judges – almost half did not report the behavior that they witnessed to anyone.

It is perhaps, though, not the people who responded to the survey that reveal the most about the courtroom atmosphere, but rather those that chose not to complete the survey, such as one court employee who replied, "I have received your survey on sexual orientation and found it to be degrading and offensive. . . . I am sure the Judicial Council could find better use of the talent, time and money that is being wasted on a minority of court personnel" (SOFS 2001: 13). That there were any individuals unwilling to complete the survey because the mere thought of doing so was repulsive and/or a waste of their time suggests that anti-Queer sentiment in the courtroom is even more pervasive than the study revealed.

In 1997, a similar but smaller study conducted by the Arizona State Bar of the Board of Governors created a *Task Force on Gay and Lesbian Issues* to assess the experiences of gays and lesbians in Arizona courtrooms (Cramer 2002). The Task Force sent surveys to 291 judges (29% response rate), 450 attorneys (29% response rate), 465 law students at one University (22% response rate), 476 law students at another University (12% response rate), and 800 Queer community members (48% response rate). The results were bleaker than the California study. Seventy seven percent of judges and lawyers reported hearing disparaging remarks about gays and lesbians, often in public areas of the courthouse. Even more law students (90%) reported hearing negative comments. Based on these findings and further evidence of discriminatory treatment (e.g. 13% of judges reported negative treatment of gays and lesbians in open court), the Task Force concluded that these incidents of negative treatment were significant and in need of being addressed via mandated education on sexual diversity for court employees. Subsequently, the State Bar added this component to an existing required course on professionalism and the Arizona Supreme Court included sexual orientation to their Ethical Rule against manifesting prejudice.

In a more general sense and much like many members of the public, gays and lesbians are most likely to find themselves in a court of law as a result of jury duty (Brower 2011). As only some jurisdictions disallow peremptory strikes based on sexual orientation, potential gay, lesbian, and bisexual jurors (and realistically trans jurors) have reason to fear unwanted "outing" or expect discrimination in the voir dire process (Shay 2014). Conversely, Queer defendants could benefit from a voir dire process that questions a potential juror's biases regarding sexuality and gender identity. Thus, the voir dire process is of great significance to the outcomes of the cases that actually result in a jury trial. As Brower (2011: 672) points out, these "experiences shape how gay people perceive the quality of justice and access to the judicial system" including, presumably, how they will be treated as defendants or victims.

The biases and discrimination that Queer people face in larger society follow them into the courtroom, especially if they are facing charges for sexual offenses. Queer sex offenders are often overcharged and, consequently, accept unfair plea deals (Mogul et al. 2011). Prosecutorial discretion is especially problematic for Queer youth who find themselves charged with statutory rape because they are not extended the "Romeo and Juliet" exception afforded to heterosexual youth by most states (Meidinger 2012).

The "Romeo and Juliet" exception is when the defendant and the victim are close in age, engaged in clearly consensual sex, and are perceived to be committed to one another – some states actually define a range of age differences that would be deemed acceptable in this sort of situation. The problem is that prosecutors are less likely to perceive Queer youth to be in "appropriate" committed relationships, and the legally defined age ranges often exclude same-sex encounters. Texas, Alabama, and California all have age range exceptions for statutory rape, but all of them explicitly apply to heterosexual youth only, meaning that Queer youth face harsher punishment for engaging in the same behaviors as their heterosexual peers (Meidinger 2012). Considering the survey findings from California and Arizona, it is safe to assume that the decisions that prosecutors make are couched in negative attitudes towards Queer citizens and are more than likely based on personal beliefs regarding what is or is not "appropriate."

A striking example of this is the Kansas case involving Matthew Limon, a developmentally disabled 18 year old (ACLU 2005; Meidinger 2012). While attending a residential school for the developmentally disabled, Limon had consensual oral sex with a young man who was 15 – just over three years younger than him. In Kansas, the Romeo and Juliet law can reduce the severity of punishment in cases of consensual sex where the victim is between 14 and 16 years old, the offender is under the age of 19, the victim and offender have no more than a four year age gap, and the victim and offender "are members of the opposite sex." Because the Romeo and Juliet law didn't apply to Limon's case solely because of the "opposite sex" distinction, he was convicted of sodomy and sentenced to 17 years and two months in prison and ordered to register as a sex offender. Had he engaged in heterosexual sex and thus able to use the Romeo and Juliet law, Limon would have served approximately 15 months for his crime and would have avoided the stigma of registering as a sex offender altogether. Limon's experience is a disheartening example of where discrimination has been literally codified in the law.

Even when laws do not discriminate between offenders, courtrooms around the globe are still shrouded in homophobia. These attitudes have a real effect on sentencing outcomes for Queer offenders, sometimes even resulting in the most severe form of punishment – the death penalty (Farr 2000; Mogul 2005; Shortnacy 2001). According to Mogul (2005), for example, 40 percent of women on death row in the United States were implied to be lesbians during their trials, no doubt because prosecutors know that some jurors are likely to hold negative attitudes towards Queer defendants, as evidenced in the findings above. In fact, jurors are three times more likely to be biased towards gay litigants than they are towards Blacks, Asians, Hispanics, and whites (Brower 2011).

It may well have been this bias that sent Bernina Mata to death row in 1999 for stabbing a man to death. Her prosecutor mentioned her sexuality during her bond hearing, before the grand jury, and during a motion to suppress evidence hearing. Additionally, the prosecution insisted that her lesbianism was the motive for the murder. Ten different witnesses were called to testify to her sexual orientation, lesbian-themed books from her home were entered as evidence, and the prosecution mentioned her sexuality 17 different times during their closing arguments (Mogul 2005). During her trial, in open court, Prosecutor Troy Owens made his intention quite clear: "We are trying to show that [Bernina Mata] has a motive to commit this crime in that she is a hard core lesbian, and that is why she reacted to Mr. Draheim's behavior in this way. A normal heterosexual woman would not be offended by such conduct as to murder" (Mogul 2005: 473).

Unfortunately, Mata's treatment in court is not unique. Characterizing female offenders as man-hating lesbians or as defying traditional gender roles (i.e. being "manly"), at least in capital cases, is well documented (Farr 2000; Mogul 2005; Shortnacy 2001). The media and courtroom descriptions of some female offenders (murderers in particular) are reminiscent of Hollywood movie trailers, such as in the case of Australian Tracey Wigginton, who was also convicted of stabbing a man to death. Upon her release from prison, one *Herald Sun* headline proclaimed: "Satanic lesbian vampire killer Tracey Wigginton terrified Australians in gruesome 1990s trial" (Hunt 2013). A basic internet search for Wigginton reveals that nearly every article and book written about Wigginton refers to her as a "lesbian vampire killer."

More recently, in 2007, similar language was used by the media to describe a group of young, Black lesbians who defended themselves against the unwanted sexual advances of Dwayne Buckle. When the girls told him they were not interested, he reportedly called them "fucking dykes" and told them that he would "fuck them straight." The women went on to say that Buckle spit and threw a cigarette at them and grabbed one of them by the throat before they defended themselves (Italiano 2007). Even Italiano's (2007) description of this case, which outlined the gory details surrounding the incident, used disparaging language about the women involved.

HEADLINE: ATTACK OF THE KILLER LESBIANS

Next thing he knew, he was encircled, beaten and knifed in the gut right there on a Greenwich Village sidewalk – by seven bloodthirsty young lesbians.

Laura Italiano, New York Post, *2007*

These descriptions are not without consequence, and lead to capital convictions in cases that would not typically be tried as such (i.e. murders of individuals, usually known intimately by the offender, by offenders with little to no prior record). In her study of media depictions of death row inmates in 1993, Farr (2000: 63) concludes that "the cases are linked through portrayals of the perpetrators as embodiments of defeminized and dehumanized female evil for whom chivalry must be forfeited and the most severe punishment delivered."

In the United States, the most famous use of a woman's lesbianism as fodder for the prosecution was the case of Aileen Wuornos, a prostitute who, between 1989 and 1990, shot and killed seven men believed to be her customers. Wuornos has become one of the most widely recognized criminals in history not just because she is one of the world's few female serial killers, but because her story became the center of a media-fueled frenzy and the topic of dozens of books, a musical opera, television programs, songs, poems, documentaries, and films, including the award-winning Hollywood movie *Monster* starring Charlize Theron. Chesney-Lind and Eliason (2006) point out that the film's depiction of Wuornos is entrenched in stereotypes about female masculinity and lesbianism, in large part to convince the audience that she is evil and unworthy of sympathy, despite the fact that the actual evidence in the case suggests that her crimes were acts of self-defense or related to violence-induced post-traumatic stress disorder. "After all," they note, "a lesbian prostitute that murders men seeking sex from her confirms many popular, heterosexist notions about the relationship between lesbianism, masculinity, and female violence" (Chesney-Lind & Eliason 2006: 39–40). Wuornos was sentenced to death and was executed by lethal injection on October 9, 2002.

Women are not alone in having their sexuality (or presumed sexuality) and gender nonconformity used as evidence against them or as speculation by the prosecution (Shortnacy 2001). Calvin Burdine's sexuality, for example, may have been the proverbial nail in his coffin. In 1983, Burdine was convicted of capital murder after a trial that lasted less than 13 hours. During the sentencing phase of the trial, the prosecutor addressed the jury, telling them that "sending a homosexual to the penitentiary certainly isn't a very bad punishment for a homosexual, and that's what he's asking you to do" (Shortnacy 2001: 347). This statement was preceded by the prosecutor failing to remove jurors that expressed homophobic attitudes and by Burdine's prior consensual sodomy conviction being entered into evidence. Burdine was sentenced to death, but did eventually have a successful appeal – not on the grounds of prosecutorial prejudice or misconduct, but because his lawyer slept through much of his short trial. Consequently, he then pleaded guilty in exchange for three life sentences (Weinstein 2003). The prosecutor's comments during trial regarding Burdine's sexual orientation and the assumption that prison is a sexual playground for Queer identified offenders speaks to the stereotypes that plague the criminal legal system, especially in the punishment stage. These assumptions and problematics will be addressed in greater detail in Chapter 5.

I was sure that the police were coming to help me. And when they arrived, they were ready to attack me. They were so quick to . . . make me the aggressor. . . . And they were like, "Somebody got stabbed" And I was like, "Yeah, I got stabbed in the face." They didn't care.

CeCe McDonald
Signorile 2014

Despite the negative experiences of Queer offenders, it is logical to conclude that as cultural attitudes regarding sexuality and gender become more progressive, the Queer community will become more apt to engage the criminal legal system when they find themselves victims to crime (Shay 2014). In general, Queer victims are now receiving more public empathy than they have in the past (Smith 2002), but this doesn't necessarily mean that they will receive equitable or appropriate treatment by the courts, especially if they choose to defend themselves from violence. The recent case of CeCe McDonald is a haunting example of a person whose victimization was altogether ignored because she made the choice to fight back against her attacker. In 2011, McDonald, a Black trans woman, was assaulted by a white woman outside of a bar as several people yelled racist and transphobic remarks at her, including "You niggers need to go back to Africa" and "Look at that boy dressed as a girl, tucking his dick in" (Erderly 2014: n.p.). Her attacker dragged her to the ground and slashed her face with a broken glass. As she tried to leave the scene, her assailant's ex-boyfriend ran after her, and McDonald fatally stabbed him with a pair of scissors. Despite the fact that McDonald's action could be seen as self-defense, she was arrested and charged with murder and, in order to avoid up to 80 years in prison, she pleaded guilty to second-degree murder and served 19 months of a 41-month sentence in a men's prison. Since her arrest, conviction, and subsequent release, McDonald has become an iconic figure in the Queer rights movement and a symbol for exposing and challenging transphobia.

Gay/trans panic

Though much of this book highlights the ways in which Queer experiences with the criminal legal system are shaped by homophobia and heteronormativity, we also must recognize that non-Queer people have attempted to use these systems of denigration to their benefit. One example of this is the "gay panic" or "trans panic" defense, which has been used by some defendants to justify violent crimes against the Queer community. The defense is a simple one – the defendant claims that the victim made unwanted sexual advances against them and, in self-defense, the defendant commits an act of violence against the victim (thus warranting a lesser charge). Though there is no data on how many times the gay or trans panic defense has been used, some suggest it has been employed approximately 45 times in the United States (Perkiss 2013). Formerly called the "homosexual panic" defense, it is thought to have been used first in the 1967 case of *People v. Rodriguez*, in which the defendant hit a man in the head (killing him) after the victim supposedly grabbed his genitals while he was urinating in an alley. The defense worked for Rodriguez, inasmuch as he was convicted of second rather than first-degree murder (Perkiss 2013). Two of the more recent and widely publicized cases where a gay or trans panic defense was introduced are those involving victims Lawrence King and Gwen Araujo, both from California.

In 2008, openly gay 15-year-old Larry King of Oxnard, California, was shot twice in the back of his head by 14-year-old classmate Brandon McInerney for supposedly flirting with him and publicly asking him to be his Valentine. The shooting occurred in the school computer lab in front of witnesses, so there was no question that McInerney was guilty of killing Larry. What was under question was whether or not he should be tried as an adult (which he was) and if he was guilty of first degree murder and a hate crime (as the prosecution contended), or if his "panic" and rage over King's advances made his offense voluntary manslaughter (as the defense contended). It was a question the jurors were apparently not equipped to answer, as it was a hung jury that resulted in a mistrial, perhaps because some of the jurors were sympathetic to McInerney and felt as though he was a victim of Larry's advances.

> Where are the civil rights of the one being taunted by another person that is cross-dressing?
> *Diane Michaels, Juror for the Brandon McInerney trial*
> Valentine Road *2013 [Film]*

Rather than face another trial, McInerney pleaded guilty to second-degree murder and was sentenced to 21 years in prison. Some of the jurors from the trial appeared at his sentencing wearing gray bracelets that read, "Save Brandon" (Barlow 2011). The King/McInerney case was tragic, and not just because a young gay boy lost his life. The case highlighted the intersections of race, as McInerney was supposedly dabbling in neo-Nazi propaganda; class, as both boys lived in extreme poverty (indeed, Larry was living in an emergency shelter at the time); and age, as the jurors struggled with the notion of sentencing a 14 year old as an adult. In many ways, both boys were victims – they had both experienced lives of violence and a failed system, and they both serve as reminders of the complexity of victimization, offending, and punishment.

Gwen Araujo is perhaps the most famous transgender murder victim that the United States has seen since the murder of Brandon Teena (see Chapter 3), in part due to the award-winning Lifetime made-for-television movie *A Girl Like Me: The Gwen Araujo Story*. In 2002, Gwen was just 17 years old when four men beat and strangled her to death and buried her in a shallow grave after discovering that she had male genitalia. Gwen had allegedly had sexual relations with two of the men – Jose Merel and Michael Magidson – whose attorneys were able to convince a second jury (the first trial ended in a hung jury) that they had been "reasonably provoked" by Gwen's "deception" (Lee 2013: 828). It is not surprising that panic defenses work in cases like Merel and Magidson, since murders of Queer people (particularly of trans folks) are often framed by the media as being the direct result of the victim's "deception." In their review of news articles concerning transgender murders between 1990 and 2005, Schilt and Westbrook (2009) found that journalists framed 56 percent of the violence to be connected to sexual encounters whereby the offender felt "tricked" or "duped" by the victim.

Both men were convicted of second-degree murder and were acquitted of the hate crime charges that had been brought against them. They are serving sentences of 15 years to life in prison. The other two men involved – Jason Cazares and Jaron Nabors – pleaded no contest and guilty, respectively, to manslaughter, and received sentences of six and eleven years. It was anger over these sentences that led to the 2006 passing of the Gwen Araujo Justice for Victims Act, which bans the use of "panic strategies" as courtroom defenses. The Act effectively made California the first state to ban the use of gay and trans panic defenses in criminal trials. A similar bill is currently being considered in New Jersey (Friedman 2014).

Sentencing enhancement through hate crime legislation

While the gay panic defense may be used as an attempt to skirt harsh punishment, federal and state hate crime laws are intended to mete out harsher punishments to those whose crimes are motivated by hate. According to the FBI's hate crime statistics, United States law enforcement agencies reported 1,402 hate crime offenses based on sexual orientation bias and 33 based on gender-identity bias in 2013, constituting approximately 21 percent of all hate crimes reported in that year. While shocking, these statistics are grossly underestimated and are at odds with other sources. While the FBI only reports that two of the hate-motivated murders in 2013 were related to sexual orientation (and zero related to gender identity), the National Coalition of Anti-Violence Programs (NCAVP 2014) reported 18 antigay or antitransgender hate-related homicides in the same year. According to the NCAVP, more than half of those victims were transgender women of color.

The Matthew Shepard and James Byrd, Jr. Hate Crimes Prevention Act (hereafter referred to as the HCPA) was passed in 2009, giving the federal government more leverage in the prosecution of crimes involving bodily harm due to someone's race, color, religion, national origin, disability, sexual orientation, and gender identity, especially where state-level hate crime laws fall short. Both of the men that the HCPA memorialized were violently murdered in 1998 – Matthew died from injuries he sustained when two men beat him and tied him to a fence post because he was a gay man, and James (who was Black) died from being tied to the back of pick-up truck by three white supremacists and dragged several miles.

Currently, there are 45 states that have their own hate crime statutes, but 15 of those states do not include sexual orientation or gender identity as protected characteristics, and most of the remaining states only recognize one or the other (Human Rights Campaign 2015a). There are 27 other countries (most of them in Europe) that consider hate crimes related to sexual orientation to be an aggravating circumstance. Spain became the first to do so in 1998 (Itaborahy & Zhu 2014), and scholars continue to urge other countries to follow suit (Prunas, Clerici, Gentile, Muccino, Veneroni, & Zoja 2014). There are 28 countries that have banned "incitement of hatred" based on sexual orientation, effectively prohibiting hate speech (Itaborahy & Zhu 2014). It is fear of this sort of legislation that has led to challenges of the constitutionality of the HCPA in the United States, including in the 2012 Michigan case of *Glenn v. Holder*.

Gary Glenn (then President of the American Family Association of Michigan) and his co-plaintiffs (all pastors at Christian churches) alleged that the HCPA violated their rights to freedom of speech in regard to their "opposition to homosexuality, homosexual activism, and the homosexual agenda" (see *Glenn v. Holder* 2012). Though the plaintiffs did not act or intend to act violently against gays or lesbians, they argued that the HCPA would cause them to be placed under unwarranted surveillance as a result of their vocal beliefs. The Attorney General's request to dismiss the case was granted, and it appears that Glenn's right to freedom of speech was not affected by the HCPA in the least, as he went on to win a seat in the Michigan House of Representatives and was coauthor of Michigan's constitutional ban on gay marriage. His website boasts that "I'll use my god-given abilities to benefit all Michigan citizens" (Glenn n.d.) – unless, it appears, if they're gay.

Criticisms of the HCPA (and similar state laws) are not, however, limited to extremists who feel that their hateful rhetoric will be threatened. Whether good or bad, hate crime laws do raise complex definitional and judicial issues that should not be ignored. Perhaps the most basic academic debate is over the very term "hate crime," as some have argued that many acts that could be considered hate crimes are not necessarily committed out of hate (an *emotion*), but as the result of one's prejudiced or biased *disposition* (Garland & Chakraborti 2012). Moreover, one could easily argue that hate is an element in some crimes that would not fit under the legal rubric of "hate crimes" – for example, someone who kills their spouse's lover.

In her overview of psychology-based objections to hate crime laws, Sullaway (2004) outlines the potential difficulties of measuring bias and intent in hate crimes as distinct or different from the bias and intent found in "non-hate" related crimes. She also points out that it is impossible to prove a causal relationship between one's prejudicial attitudes and actions so, even if you use one of the psychological assessments of bias that are available to measure a defendant's disposition, it wouldn't necessarily prove the commission of a hate crime, per se.

Meyer (2014) makes a compelling argument for the rejection of hate crime laws based on the misleading message they send to the public – that is, that the criminal legal system is a solution to prejudicial violence, which, as described throughout this book, has long been meted out by the state. Hate crime laws, he points out, only serve to expand the prosecutorial power of the state, which is counter to the goals of the Queer rights movement and to the reduction of social inequality. Anti-Queer violence is often couched in intersectional issues like race and class, thus the narrow focus of hate crime laws ignores the gamut of variables that determines who is at greatest risk of being a victim of such crimes. Moreover, it is the people most at risk of being a hate crime victim – that is, impoverished Queer (especially transgender) people of color – who will be disproportionately affected by the expansion of surveillance powers police are afforded through the HCPA. These worries echo trepidation regarding changes to hate crime legislation in the United States. Buist and Stone (2014) highlight Strout's (2012) research that turned attention to the concern of two prominent transgender rights groups, *Black and Pink* and the *Sylvia Rivera Law Project*, who have both contended that changing legislation will do little to combat a change in behavior or attitudes. In other words, "what the law says will not change the condition of vulnerability" (Strout 2012, as cited in Buist & Stone 2014: 39).

Regardless of the utility of hate crime statutes, it is clear that something must be done. In 2014, the United States saw the murders of no fewer than 13 transgender women (all but one of them women of color), and by the end of January 2015, two more were found dead (Human Rights Campaign 2015b). These numbers, of course, do not include those deaths not reported and do not include trans men or sexual minorities. In a survey of over 90,000 LGBT people in the European Union, 6 percent of respondents had experienced physical or sexual violence against them in last 12 months as a result of their actual or perceived sexual or gender identity (European Union Agency for Fundamental Rights 2014). Hate crime statutes are at best symbolic, and serve in no way to prevent violence against the Queer community. Laws do not deter crime and, as described in the cases above, only sometimes serve to punish those who commit them.

Recommended viewing

A Girl Like Me: The Gwen Araujo Story, 2006. [Film] Directed by Agnieszka Holland. USA: Braun Entertainment Group.

Aileen: Life and Death of a Serial Killer, 2003. [Film] Directed by Nick Broomfield & Joan Churchill. USA: Lafayette Films.

Licensed to Kill, 1997. [Film] Directed by Arthur Dong. USA: Deep Focus Productions.

Monster, 2003. [Film] Directed by Patty Jenkins. USA: Media 8 Entertainment.

Out in the Night, 2014. [Film] Directed by Blair Doroshwalther. USA: ITVS.
Outrage, 2009. [Film] Directed by Kirby Dick. USA: Chain Camera Pictures.
The Case Against 8, 2014. [Film] Directed by Ben Cotner & Ryan White. USA: HBO.
The New Black, 2013. [Film] Directed by Yoruba Richen. USA: Promised Land Film.
Valentine Road, 2013. [Film] Directed by Marta Cunningham. USA: BMP Films.

References

ACLU. 2005. *Limon v. Kansas: Case background.* Accessed from https://www.aclu.org/lgbt-rights_hiv-aids/limon-v-kansas-case-background.

Barlow, Z. 2011. *Brandon McInerney sentenced to 21 years in prison for killing Larry King. Ventura County Star*, December 19. Accessed from http://www.vcstar.com/news/local-news/crime/judge-sentences-brandon-mcinerney-to-21-years-in.

Brower, Todd. 2011. *Twelve angry – and sometimes alienated – men: The experiences and treatment of lesbians and gay men during jury service. Drake Law Review, 59*: 669–706.

Buist, C.L. & Stone, C. 2014. *Transgender victims and offenders: Failures of the United States criminal justice system and the necessity of a queer criminology. Critical Criminology, 22*, (1): 35–47.

Burdge, H., Licona, A.C., & Hyemingway, Z.T. 2014. *LGBTQ youth of color: Discipline disparities, school push-out, and the school-to-prison pipeline.* San Francisco, CA: Gay-Straight Alliance Network.

Chesney-Lind, M. & Eliason, M. 2006. *From invisible to incorrigible: The demonization and marginalization of women and girls. Crime, Media, Culture, 2*, (1): 29–47.

Collins, Jeffery. 2014. *Latta, South Carolina rallies for fired lesbian police chief Crystal Moore. Huffington Post*, July 13. Accessed from http://www.huffingtonpost.com/2014/07/13/latta-fired-lesbian-police-chief-_n_5583048.html.

Cramer, A.C. 2002. *Discovering and addressing sexual orientation bias in Arizona's legal system. Journal of Gender, Social Policy & the Law, 11*, (1): 25–37.

Csete, J. & Cohen, J. 2010. *Health benefits of legal services for criminalized populations: The case of people who use drugs, sex workers and sexual and gender minorities. Journal of Law, Medicine & Ethics, 38*, (4): 816–831.

Erderly, S.R. 2014. *The transgender crucible. Rolling Stone*, July 30. Accessed from http://www.rollingstone.com/culture/news/the-transgender-crucible-20140730.

Erlanger, S. & Sayare, S. 2013. *Protests against same-sex marriage bill intensify in France. The New York Times*, April 22. Accessed from http://www.nytimes.

com/2013/04/23/world/europe/in-france-opposition-to-same-sex-marriage-bill-grows.html?pagewanted=all&_r=0.

Espinoza, R. 2007. *A global gaze: Lesbian, gay, bisexual, transgender and intersex grantmaking in the global south and east.* New York, NY: Funders for Lesbian and Gay Issues.

European Union Agency for Fundamental Rights. 2014. *EU LGBT survey: European Union lesbian, gay, bisexual and transgender survey.* Luxembourg: Publications Office of the European Union.

Farr, K.A. 2000. *Defeminizing and dehumanizing female murderers: Depictions of lesbians on death row. Women & Criminal Justice, 11,* (1): 49–66.

Ferrigno, L. 2014. *Attack after same-sex marriage shines light on Michigan hate crime law. CNN,* April 7. Accessed from http://www.cnn.com/2014/04/05/us/michigan-hate-crime-attack/.

Friedman, M. 2014. *N.J. lawmaker seeks to ban "gay panic" murder defense.* NJ.com, December 26. Accessed from http://www.nj.com/politics/index.ssf/2014/12/nj_lawmaker_seeks_to_ban_gay_panic_murder_defense.html.

Garland, J. & Chakraborti, N. 2012. *Divided by a common concept? Assessing the implications of different conceptualizations of hate crime in the European Union. European Journal of Criminology, 9,* (10): 38–51.

Glenn, G. n.d. Gary's Pledge. Accessed from www.garyglenn.us/pledge.

Glenn v. Holder. 690 F. 3d 417 (2012).

Himmelstein, K.E.W. & Bruckner, H. 2011. *Criminal-justice and school sanctions against nonheterosexual youth: A national longitudinal study. Pediatrics, 127,* (1): 49–57.

Human Rights Campaign. 2015a. *Maps of state laws and policies: State hate crimes.* Accessed from http://www.hrc.org/state_maps.

Human Rights Campaign. 2015b. *A national crisis: Anti-transgender violence.* Accessed from http://hrc-assets.s3-website-us-east-1.amazonaws.com//files/assets/resources/HRC_AntiTransgenderViolence.pdf.

Hunt, E. 2013. *Satanic lesbian vampire killer Tracey Wigginton terrified Australians in gruesome 1990s trial. Herald Sun,* March 5. Accessed from http://www.heraldsun.com.au/news/law-order/evil-act-of-a-satanic-lesbian-vampire-killer/story-fnat7jnn-1226590831480.

Itaborahy, L.P. & Zhu, J. 2014. *State-sponsored homophobia. A world survey of laws: Criminalization, protection & recognition of same-sex love.* Geneva: International Lesbian Gay Bisexual Trans and Intersex Association.

Italiano, L. 2007. *Attack of the killer lesbians. New York Post,* April 12. Accessed from http://nypost.com/2007/04/12/attack-of-the-killer-lesbians/.

Keck, T.M. 2009. *Beyond backlash: Assessing the impact of judicial decisions on LGBT rights. Law & Society Review, 43,* (1): 151–185.

Kosciw, J.G., Greytak, E.A., Palmer, N.A., & Boeson, M.J. 2014. *The 2013 national school climate survey: The experiences of lesbian, gay, bisexual and transgender youth in our nation's school.* New York, NY: Gay, Lesbian and Straight Education Network.

Lee, C. 2013. *Masculinity on Trial: Gay Panic in the Criminal Courtroom. Southwestern Law Review, 42:* 817–831.

Meidinger, M.H. 2012. *Peeking under the covers: Taking a closer look at prosecutorial decision-making involving queer youth and statutory rape. Boston College Journal of Law & Social Justice, 32,* (2): 421–451.

Meyer, D. 2014. *Resisting hate crime discourse: Queer and intersectional challenges to neoliberal hate crime laws. Critical Criminology, 22:* 113–125.

Mogul, J.L. 2005. *The dykier, the butcher, the better: The state's use of homophobia and sexism to execute women in the United States. New York City Law Review, 8:* 473–493.

Mogul, J.L., Ritchie, A.J., & Whitlock, K. 2011. *Queer (in)justice: The criminalization of LGBT people in the United States.* Boston, MA: Beacon Press.

Monster, 2003. [Film] Directed by Patty Jenkins. USA: Media 8 Entertainment.

National Coalition of Anti-Violence Programs. 2014. *Lesbian, gay, bisexual, transgender, queer, and HIV-affected hate violence in 2013.* New York, NY: Gay and Lesbian Anti-violence Project, INC.

People v. Rodriguez. 256 Cal. App. 2d 663 (1967).

Perkiss, D.A. 2013. *A new strategy for neutralizing the gay panic defense at trial: Lessons from the Lawrence King case. UCLA Law Review, 60,* (3): 778–824.

Pew Research Center. 2013. *Gay marriage around the world.* December 19. Accessed from http://www.pewforum.org/2013/12/19/gay-marriage-around-the-world-2013/.

Potts, A. 2014. *France had 78% rise in anti-gay incidents in the year it legalized gay marriage.* Gay Star News, May 14. Accessed from http://www.gaystarnews.com/article/france-had-78-rise-anti-gay-incidents-year-it-legalized-gay-marriage140514.

Prunas, A., Clerici, C.A., Gentile, G., Muccino, E., Veneroni, L., & Zoja, R. 2014. *Transphobic murders in Italy: An overview of homicides in Milan (Italy) in the past two decades (1993–2012). Journal of Interpersonal Violence:* 1–14.

Schilt, K. & Westbrook, L. 2009. *Doing gender, doing heteronormativity: "Gender normals," transgender people, and the social maintenance of heterosexuality. Gender & Society, 23,* (4): 440–464.

Sexual Orientation Fairness Committee. 2001. *Sexual orientation fairness in the California courts: Final report of the Sexual Orientation Fairness Subcommittee of the Judicial Council's Access and Fairness Advisory Committee.* Published in California.

Shay, G. 2014. *In the box: Voir dire on LGBT issues in changing times. Harvard Journal of Law & Gender, 37*: 407–457.

Shortnacy, M.B. 2001. *Guilty and gay, a recipe for execution in American courtrooms: Sexual orientation as a tool for prosecutorial misconduct in death penalty cases. American University Law Review, 51,* (2): 309–365.

Signorile, M. 2014. *CeCe McDonald, transgender activist, recalls hate attack, manslaughter case. Huffington Post,* February 22. Accessed from http://www.huffingtonpost.com/2014/02/22/cece-mcdonald-manslaughter-case_n_4831677.html.

Smith, A. 2002. *The complex uses of sexual orientation in criminal court. Journal of Gender, Social Policy & the Law, 11,* (1): 101–115.

Snapp, S.D., Hoenig, J.M., Fields, A., & Russell, S.T. 2014. *Messy, butch, and queer: LGBTQ youth and the school-to-prison pipeline. Journal of Adolescent Research, 30,* (1): 57–82.

Strout, J. 2012. The *Massachusetts transgender equal rights bill: Formal legal equality in a transphobic system. Harvard Journal of Law & Gender, 35*: 515–521.

Sullaway, M. 2004. *Psychological perspectives on hate crime laws. Psychology, Public Policy, and Law, 10,* (3): 250–292.

Weinstein, H. 2003. *Inmate in Texas sleeping-lawyer case pleads guilty. Los Angeles Times,* June 20. Accessed from http://articles.latimes.com/2003/jun/20/nation/na-sleep20.

5

QUEER CRIMINOLOGY AND CORRECTIONS

While incarcerated, Queer people face additional barriers that must be addressed. Much like any person who is serving time in jail or prison, Queer inmates are often forgotten and their needs ignored. The explanation for this is often couched within an argument for punishment – the individual has committed a crime and broken the social contract, therefore the offender must be punished. Law-abiding citizens may contend that they are not obligated to concern themselves with the rights of an offender when the assumption is that the offender's behavior failed to respect the boundaries of society. This argument is problematic for several reasons. Theoretically speaking, the correctional literature has paid special attention to four major theories of punishment: Retribution, deterrence, rehabilitation, and incapacitation. It can be argued that each of these theories are applied in tandem and in varying degrees when courts punish convicted offenders, but make no mistake, especially since the 1970s and the war on drugs, the United States primarily incapacitates its offenders – incarcerate them and forget them is the prevailing sentiment. So it should come as no surprise that to the majority of citizens, the incarcerated are easy to forget, no matter what injustices they face while under the control of the state.

There is little to no information on the specific crimes that Queer people commit, but we contend that Queer people commit the same crimes as any non-Queer-identifying person. However, there should be special consideration given to the social impact that Queer youth and adults experience based solely on their sexual and/ or gender orientation, such as young people being kicked out of their homes, schools, being fired from their jobs, evicted by their landlords, denied health care, and so on that may have a significant impact on Queer offenders. For instance, as we briefly touched on in Chapter 3, LGBTQ youth face being kicked out of their homes by bigoted family members, without any alternative housing, these young people often find themselves on the streets (see Holsinger & Hodge 2014; Majd, Marksamer, & Reyes 2009; Moodie-Mills & Gilbert 2014). Street life can lead to a broad range of criminal acts, from minor vagrancy offenses all the way up to felonious behavior such as prostitution or theft. Once in the system, the likelihood that one will remain in the system increases exponentially. Further, because Queer people may lack the assistance and resources at home and within their communities, this lack of support may lead them to recidivate at higher rates than heterosexual offenders.

Much of the current research on Queer offenders is couched within the transgender and gay populations in prison. Therefore, this chapter will rely and focus heavily on the literature on those groups. However, before we turn our focus to Queer people's experiences in jails and prisons, we want to take a moment to address other correctional topics that must not be overlooked. First, although most of the research focuses on punishment behind bars, this is not to say, of course, that Queer people are not found in all stages of the correctional process – as offenders they certainly may be punished by serving their sentences in the community. If this is the case, probation officers who are already tirelessly overworked would require the appropriate training in order to understand, at the very least, the unique experiences of Queer people under their correctional supervision. For instance, and perhaps especially salient for younger Queer people in the system, they may have more difficulty obtaining housing not only because of their minority status, but because they have been kicked out of their family home. Simply put, Queer people may have heightened difficulty in having familial and/or community support because they are sexual or gender minorities.

We also cannot ignore the hatred and discrimination that Queer people face around the globe. As Chapter 2 indicated in great detail, there is a real concern regarding the human rights and civil liberties of Queer people and the prejudiced attitudes and discriminatory behavior is heightened when countries have legal bans and, in turn, legal sanctions up to and including death for "homosexuality." For instance, to revisit Cameroon's "anti-homosexuality law," participants in the Human Rights Watch (2013) report noted that prisons guards (warders) beat them while in custody. One victim, "G.M." reported being stripped naked, having her or his head shaved, and being waterboarded while correctional authorities sang anti-gay songs (Human Rights Watch 2013). Unfortunately, even in more "progressive" countries like the United States, Queer people are targeted based on their sexual orientation and gender identity as well. What is lesser known, however, is that Queer correctional officers also experience victimization.

Much like our discussion on Queer law enforcement officers in Chapter 2's section on "Queer and blue," Queer correctional officers face the same difficulties on the job, and in essence, as officers of the law, they too, are law enforcement officials. However, here we mention specific research and incidents regarding Queer-identified correctional officers only. First, it should be noted that there is little research that has been conducted specifically on prison guards who are Queer. What information that is available has highlighted court proceedings of gay-identified correctional officers who have sued their departments for having been terminated from their jobs because of their sexual orientation, or who have quit their jobs because of the profound amount of harassment they have faced and lack of support that has been offered to them. Two cases in particular are those of Robert Ranger in Canada and Kristin King in the United States.

Correctional officer Robert Ranger, who spent four years working in the Ottawa-Carleton Detention Centre, filed suit based on his continued harassment at the hands of fellow officers. Ranger told the Grievance Settlement Board that during his tenure at the facility he was taunted and the focus of antigay jokes and slurs. Facing such harassment led to depression and anxiety. Although the board awarded him nearly $100,000 in compensation, the psychological impact of the experiences remained. During this time, he was offered employment in other areas in corrections, but he felt as though he was being set up for failure because they were jobs that he had little to no knowledge of or skill for (*Canadian Press* 2013).

In the United States, former Maine correctional officer Kristin King, the only out lesbian guard working the night shift at Downeast Correctional Facility, filed suit noting that she was differentially disciplined and that the "old boy culture of disrespect for women" was pervasive in the prison and therefore made it increasingly difficult for King to perform her duties. Much like Ranger's lawsuit, King cited growing anxiety and panic attacks, migraine headaches, and sleeplessness brought on by stress from her mistreatment (Mack 2013).

In addition to the discrimination and harassment that Ranger and King identified experiencing, it is important to draw attention to the story of Mandi Camille Hauwert, a former controlman in the Navy, and who is currently a correctional officer at San Quentin prison and recently transitioned from male to female while on the job. In an opinion editorial in *The Advocate*, she tells her story, indicating that her transition was slow going, but that for the most part her supervisor and prison administrators were supportive. However, there was still a fear and anxiety that Hauwert faced as she wondered how the inmates and her fellow officers would respond. She admits, "I thought I would be fired or dead within a month" (Hauwert 2015). Interestingly, Hauwert revealed that it has not been the inmates who have had issues with her transition, even noting that the inmates continue to show her respect. Instead, it had been her fellow officers who were the most intolerant of her transition, commenting that one officer told her that he could not recognize her as a woman because of his religious beliefs. In addition, she continues to deal with some officers calling her by incorrect pronouns and others who refer to her as "it" and "tranny."

Some may argue that it is a given that inmates respect the officer because, regardless of sex or gender presentation, the guard is still their primary agent of social control. Of course, we know this is not always the case. Ask any correctional officer who has been verbally or physically attacked – they are not necessarily automatically respected because of their position of power within the prison. The administration, in this case, was supportive of Hauwert's transition, but her peers were her biggest source of anxiety; and, as indicated in the King case, the old boys network (read: patriarchal, hierarchical, and masculinist) reinforces stereotypes about gender presentation and, in turn, breeds misunderstanding, malcontent, and mistreatment.

Moving forward, we turn the focus to specific issues associated with the experiences of Queer people in jails and prisons – some of whom are offenders and some of whom are detained yet not considered criminals – namely immigrant asylum seekers abroad. First, we will begin with how Queer people are housed and classified in prisons and how the current policies continue to be problematic and damaging to Queer-identified people who are incarcerated. We will then discuss medical issues and the right to transition, followed by an account of rapes and sexual assaults committed against Queer offenders.

Housing and classification

The American Bar Association's *Standards On Treatment of Prisoners* states in section 23, 2.2 Part C that "classification and housing decisions, including assignment to particular cells and cellmates, take account of a prisoner's *gender*, age, offense, criminal history, institutional behavior, escape history, *vulnerability*, mental health, and *special needs*, and whether the prisoner is a pretrial detainee" (ABA 2010, emphasis added). As indicated in the emphasized portions of this statement on prisoner classification, the ABA denotes the importance of considering gender in prisoner classification – this is an extremely important point and brings us back to the importance of language as discussed in Chapter 1. First, as you may recall, there is a tendency to conflate the terms sex and gender by incorrectly assuming that these two things are one in the same. However, we know that they are indeed *not* one in the same – remember, sex is a biological distinction, while gender is a social construction. When you are asked to fill out a form that instructs you to identify your gender, then that form has likely conflated the terms sex and gender. The credit card company is not interested in whether or not your gender expression is consistent with your biological sex, they simply want to know if you are legally male or female (we understand that this concept is addressing binaries rather than a sex continuum, but, for this example, the binary examples are necessary).

Therefore, when the ABA states that classification should be based on *gender*, they have conflated the terms in a manner that should be to the benefit of transgender inmates. Today, transgender inmates are classified based on their biological sex, *not* their gender identity, but, according to the ABA, they should in fact be classified by their gender identity. Regardless of the intentionality of the suggested standard, language does matter. Therefore the argument here, if this statement is interpreted literally, is that transgender inmates should be classified (and therefore housed) in a prison that represents their gender, not their sex. Conversely, the Bureau of Prisons does clearly ask for sex on their intake forms, thus there needs to be more education and clarity with regards to how inmates will be classified, and in general a better overall understanding of the differences between the two terms.

One of the major concerns within the corrections branch of the criminal legal system regarding Queer offenders is how to house and classify them once they are in the institution. In general, corrections has a problematic history of prisoner housing and classification with other populations as well, namely the elderly and the mentally ill or handicapped. The majority of jails and prisons are ill equipped to deal with special populations. Health care is available, but often sparse and lacking specialization, outside staffing are often volunteers who, even when qualified, are not readily available, and corrections officers and administrators lack the training necessary to communicate with and understand the needs of incarcerated men and women who require specialized care. What's more, Queer-identified prisoners often require additional protection while incarcerated and indeed are at a higher risk for victimization.

Transgender prisoners face unique challenges that other incarcerated people do not experience. Therefore, in addition to the same concerns that most if not all prisoners experience, such as alienation, isolation, and fear, trans prisoners may experience these emotions at a heightened level. In many prisons within the United States, the Department of Corrections (DOC) classifies prisoners based on their biological sex plus their stage of reassignment – meaning that regardless of how someone may present or how long they have taken hormones, if the individual has not had medical sex reassignment surgery, they will be placed in a prison that mirrors their biological sex. Psychologically, this can be damaging to the incarcerated person as well as being problematic for them regarding both physical safety as well as overall health, depending on the approved prescription of hormones they are allowed and/or counselling that is provided to them. Further, many prisons choose to isolate the trans inmate under the guise of protection, yet this seclusion, which is essentially administrative segregation, is problematic because this is often regarded as a punishment for inmates rather than protection (Colopy 2012).

In any case, this "protection" via segregation has become commonplace in jails and prisons across the United States, even though research has shown that prolonged isolation in prison has numerous psychological effects including, but not limited to, paranoia, inability to control emotions, increased risk of suicide, and hallucinations. In most prisons, solitary confinement or segregation isolates the incarcerated in their single cells for up to 23 hours per day. In fact, research on segregation has spawned the development of what is referred to as Security or Special Housing Unit (SHU) Syndrome. Perkinson's (1994) article on California's supermax prison, Pelican Bay, highlighted Grassian's (1983) findings that 80 percent of inmates suffered from some form of SHU syndrome, "in which they become mentally ill or their preexisting conditions are severely exacerbated" (Perkinson 1994: 120). Collins (2004: 16) drew attention to the difficulty of assessing symptoms related to prisoner segregation, but commented "that at least two courts have recognized that conditions of confinement in an ECU [Extended Control Unit] can lead to serious mental injury for some inmates."

Conversely, some research has argued that solitary confinement and segregation may not lead to the long-term psychological damage that others have purported. For example, in a one-year longitudinal study of restrictive housing in the Colorado DOC, O'Keefe, Klebe, Stucker, Sturm, and Leggett (2011) found that while participants did experience symptoms that were consistent with SHU syndrome, some of those symptoms were present before their isolation, and that, in other cases, symptoms improved over time. Hanson (2011) noted that these findings were consistent with her belief that many of the people who are housed in segregated units have psychological problems before they are placed there. What must be considered and made perfectly clear is that transgender inmates are not being placed in isolation because they have displayed harmful behavior or have been diagnosed with a mental illness; rather they are being placed there simply because of their gender identity. Thus, the broader literature on the effects of solitary confinement may not be directly applicable to our understanding of its effects on transgender inmates. Moreover, Hanssens, Moodie-Mills, Ritchie, Spade, and Vaid (2014: 21) argue that, beyond the detrimental emotional and physical effects, protective custody also limits an inmate's "access to education, work, and program opportunities . . . essential for mental health as well as achieving good time credit and being paroled." Further still, the Prison Rape Elimination Act (PREA) of 2003 restricts segregating an inmate in order to keep them safe, even if officials believe that segregating an individual will keep them safe from the risk of being sexually abused (Browne, Hastings, Kall, & diZerega 2015; Moodie-Mills & Gilbert 2014).

Quite simply, correctional officials have little to no idea what to do with incarcerated Queer folks. This is in some ways understandable as the incarcerated population of self-identified LGBTQ offenders is significantly smaller than heterosexual offenders. As of 2013, there were just under seven million (6,899,000) people under correctional supervision in the United States (Glaze & Kaeble 2014). If we were to approximate that Queer people make up 10 percent of that population, then that would equate to less than 700,000 LGBTQ people who are serving sentences either in the community, in jails, or in state or federal prisons. This statistic, 700,000 people, is no number to scoff at, but we must remember a few things: (1) If we are to enumerate this as it relates to biologically born males and females, we could estimate that over 90 percent of the 700,000 are male. (2) We cannot assume that all of these estimated offenders are open about their sexuality. Certainly, we can also assume that even if they were out in their personal lives, once they are in jail or prison it would most likely behoove them to hide their sexuality, as research has already evidenced the increased likelihood that Queer people will be victimized in prison – we also recognize that this is easier said than done for some. (3) The prison population in the United States alone is approximately 2.3 million men and women, which would decrease the possible number of Queer people in our jails and prisons to approximately 230,000. (4) There are over 3,000 jails in the United States and over 1,800 prisons in the United States that house offenders – therefore, on any given day, thousands of prisoners are held in thousands of institutions ranging from over 2,000 prisoners in the entire state of Wyoming (a scarcely populated state), to over 130,000 in California. Therefore, one would expect that California would be more equipped to address the special needs of Queer inmates than Wyoming would. However, regardless of size, or the inability to accurately assess just how many Queer inmates we have in the United States (especially transgender inmates) it is the responsibility of correctional officials to protect vulnerable populations while incarcerated.

We must also note that given the examples in the preceding chapters it is entirely possible, and is safe to assume, that Queer people are disproportionately incarcerated and their population in prison may indeed surpass their percentage in society more broadly. However, because of the poor or entirely nonexistent record keeping regarding Queer offenders and subsequently Queer inmates, this is difficult if not impossible to determine with complete certainty.

In addition to Queer people being a population who are particularly susceptible to victimization in jails and prisons, the disproportionate population of juvenile offenders may be the most vulnerable to this victimization. For instance, Majd et al. (2009) highlighted the 2006 case of *R.G. v. Koller* where three Queer youth petitioned the federal district court for abuses they experienced while under the custody of the Hawai'i Youth Correctional Facility. The court found in the plaintiffs' favor and indicated that correctional authorities failed to protect the juveniles from physical and psychological abuse, isolated the juveniles under the guise of protecting them, did not adequately train officials in order to protect the juveniles, failed to provide appropriate numbers of staff, supervisors, or an acceptable grievance system, and did not have an accurate classification system in place that protected vulnerable juveniles in their facility.

This returns us to the discussion of segregation and isolation as a means of protecting Queer inmates. While the debate will continue regarding segregation's long-term effect on inmates, we must understand that we simply do not currently have conclusive evidence to support this. However, there is no denying that some inmates do indeed suffer long after they have been released from segregation and released from prison. In their study on LGBT girls in the juvenile justice system, Holsinger and Hodge (2014: 5) contend that we should punish the attackers and not the victims by putting them in isolation. They, along with others such as Moodie-Mills and Gilbert (2014), reaffirm PREA standards that express that juveniles should not be isolated as protection. Further, they report on the girls who participated in their study feeling as though they were targeted by officials based solely on their sexual orientation, and, in turn, they were differentially punished by officers and singled out in group sessions about their relationships.

With the disproportionate numbers of Queer youth in the juvenile justice system, it is imperative to develop and implement regulations and safety standards to decrease and eliminate the victimization they experience because of their sexual and/or gender identity. Moodie-Mills and Gilbert (2014) in their report, *Restoring Justice: A Blueprint for Ensuring Fairness, Safety, and Supportive Treatment of LGBT Youth in the Juvenile Justice System*, note that 80 percent of juvenile justice officials believe that safety for LGBT juveniles is a major problem and more than half of correctional officials were aware of Queer youth being mistreated based on their sexual orientation or gender identity. Based on their findings, Moodie-Mills and Gilbert (2014: 7) suggest that considerations be made based on sexual orientation and/ or gender identity and that housing and classifying "decisions based on placement should be individualized based on youth's physical and emotional well-being and their own perspective about where they will be most secure."

An interesting and unique example of housing and classification of Queer people can be found in a California men's jail – L.A. Men's Central Jail has designated a wing of the jail for gay and transgender inmates only. The jail itself has been criticized for being in disrepair and some have called for it to be demolished and rebuilt, but as one of the largest jails in the country, housing at times nearly 5,000 inmates, that argument may continue to fall on deaf ears as budget availability is the difference maker (Editorial Board 2015). Currently, the "gay wing" of L.A. Men's Central prisons houses approximately 400 gay and trans inmates and is currently the only jail that offers such in the country (Ucar 2014).

Ucar (2014) indicates that the general population in the jail represents more violent offenses than the gay and trans inmates in the gay wing, with the majority of them committing either drug offenses (31%) or burglary or theft (32%). Gay and trans inmates are also escorted throughout the prison for added protection, and while this is an important move towards housing and classification that may indeed protect this vulnerable population, these housing and classification systems are not without their own set of problems. First and foremost, the way in which officials determine classification is rife with stereotypes and lacks any evidence of knowledge or understanding of Queer life; housing and classification within the gay wing, referred to as "K6G" is done by a "classification officer" who will ask the inmate questions about gay culture in order to determine her or his acceptance into the wing. An example question might be, can you "name a local gay bar?" If the inmate answers the question correctly, the classification officer will ask a "tougher follow-up question, such as, 'what's the cover charge'" (Ucar 2014).

Filmmaker Duncan Roy, who was held in the wing for nearly three months, commented that the only items being smuggled into the gay wing illegally would be "dresses and bras." In fact, as the article details, nearly every gay stereotype is played out in the wing from fashion shows to making illegal sewing needles (as opposed to prison weapons often called shanks). In addition to the stereotypical questions and activities in the wing, classification officers are often referred to as having "really good gay-dar" (Ucar 2014). However, despite the problems associated with this, the possibility of keeping this population safe from attack by other inmates is worthy of discussion.

Similar to the classification system in Men's Central Jail, on a more global scale, migrants who are in immigration detention centers also face issues proving their sexual orientation or gender identity if they choose to undergo what are referred to as "credibility assessments" that are used for LGBTI asylum seekers to ascertain one's sexual orientation and/or gender identity (Tabak & Levitan 2014). Credibility assessments used in this exploration were also considered stereotypical and also relied on "Westernized" ideas of what constitutes being gay. For example, in 2004, the US Board of Immigration Appeals affirmed an immigration judge who found that even though a Mexican man identified as gay, his appearance was not stereotypically gay enough to warrant protection (Tabak & Levitan 2014).

> When detention authorities either engage in or fail to make appropriate measures to respond to physical and sexual violence directed at LGBTI detainees, their actions clearly violate the prohibition of torture or cruel, inhuman, or degrading treatment as defined by applicable human rights instruments.
>
> *Tabak & Levitan 2014: 28*

Medical care and the right to transition

The rights and safety of trans-identified prisoners are real issues within the US criminal legal system as it can be (and has been) argued that denial of treatment up to and including sex reassignment surgery is a violation of the Eighth Amendment's protection from cruel and unusual punishment. Colopy (2012) indeed has noted that the World Professional Association of Transgender Health's (WPATH) Standards of Care argues for what is referred to as the full treatment series for trans inmates that includes psychotherapy, hormone therapy, and sex reassignment surgery. However, what remains especially problematic when researching trans inmates is that we are simply unaware of the number of trans inmates that are in our system. Estimates have been anywhere from 2–400 in any given state prison not including trans populations in jails. Certainly states with higher rates of incarcerations, such as California or New York, would most likely see an increase in trans prisoners (Brown 2009).

Before we go into more detail about medical concerns and transitioning in the Department of Corrections in the United States, let us first discuss the Eighth Amendment and unpack how denial of treatment and, as previously mentioned, specialized classification can violate prisoners' rights. It is oft forgotten that when an individual is sentenced, whether that is probation or incarceration, the *sentence* is the punishment. There should be *no additional punishment* that the offender faces while serving the sentence – therefore any pains of punishment that are in addition to the original sentence may in fact violate human rights protections against cruel and unusual punishment as stated in the Constitution. These additional punishments do not include punishments that are meted out based on the behavior of the offender. For instance, if an incarcerated person has broken rules within the prison or while on probation, correctional authorities are within their rights to punish her or him based on established approved protocol, but even still those punishments should never inflict additional harms against the person that are "grossly disproportionate" to the crime; that are "totally without penalogical justification," that "involve the unnecessary and wanton infliction of pain," and that are "inconsistent with 'evolving standards of decency'" (Dolovich 2009: 884, citing several cases. See *Coker v. Georgia; Gregg v. Georgia; Trop v. Dulles; Kennedy v. Louisiana; Furman v. Georgia*).

What's more, the actual punishment that is imposed also cannot be cruel and unusual. Take for example the death penalty – although we agree that the death penalty is cruel and unusual punishment in and of itself – there are ways by which to enforce this penalty that use the least invasive and the most humane methods (Dolovich 2009). Dolovich (2009: 885) continues by noting: "Indeed any harm prisoners suffer at the hands of the state while incarcerated is typically wholly unrelated to their original offense." Therefore, we absolutely must consider how denial of proper housing, classification, medical treatment, and transition can be considered Eighth Amendment violations.

First, as discussed earlier, by denying proper housing and classification once in prison, this allows for an already vulnerable inmate to be additionally susceptible to violent victimization. Next, instead of addressing the needs of this unique population, many institutions choose to isolate Queer inmates under the guise of protection. Yet again, as mentioned, this may have detrimental and long-lasting psychological effects on them. Finally, denial of medical treatment or medicine can also result in cruel and unusual punishment because lack of proper medical attention or prescriptions can be both physically and mentally damaging. We must also consider that because there is a class issue within our prisons, there is a distinct possibility that trans folks may not have been medically diagnosed with gender dysphoria (discussed below) or have been medically prescribed hormones or other drugs necessary for their transition prior to their incarceration. Indeed, many trans people obtain their drugs illegally because they do not have the means to seek a professional or afford the proper medication (Lenning & Buist 2012).

This problem is illuminated by the case of Dee Farmer, an incarcerated transgender woman who petitioned the court because, although she dressed as a woman, underwent estrogen treatment, and had breast implants prior to her sentencing, she was sent to a maximum security men's prison in Indiana. Upon arrival, Farmer was held at knifepoint and raped. Responding to her assault, Farmer filed a lawsuit against the "Bureau of Prisons director, the regional director, and other officials, alleging that they knew she would be sexually assaulted at USP-Terre Haute due to her feminine appearance" (Margolin 2014). Eventually, Farmer's suit was selected by the Supreme Court to be one of the less than 1 percent of indigent cases they would hear in 1994 and found in her favor, indicating that prison officials demonstrate "deliberate indifference" if she or he "recklessly disregards a substantial risk of to the prisoner" (ACLU 2012; *Farmer v. Brennan*, 1984).

The core of the mistreatment, harassment, and violence facing transgender people stems from this fundamental theme in the way the public doubts and denies us our true selves.
–Mara Keisling, National Center for Transgender Equality
Bell 2014

Another major issue is that in most prisons, transgender inmates must be diagnosed with gender identity disorder before they are allowed any medical care or to maintain a drug protocol (Brown 2009). Again, this may be an additional fence to jump for trans inmates, as we could contend that many are unable to access or maintain legal and/or medically supervised hormone treatments. The issue of diagnoses highlights a distinct double standard that only trans inmates seem to face. If, for example, a diabetic inmate was unable to afford insulin prior to incarceration, we do not deny that medication to her or him once incarcerated. Why? Because correctional institutions have a legal obligation to provide reasonable medical care to inmates. Thus, trans inmates are clearly facing discriminatory medical care and, thus, are facing cruel and unusual punishment. Further, while research has continued to use language such as GID (gender identity disorder), using the term "disorder" labels trans folks as having a mental condition – certainly the language itself suggests that the person has something wrong with them. Buist and Stone (2014: 11) cite Shelley (2009) indicating, "clinical discourses and diagnostic criteria actually reflect in a negative sense the social injustices that trans people face. . . ." Recently, there has been a move to eliminate the term from the diagnostic and statistical manual, replacing Gender Identity Disorder with Gender Dysphoria (GD), which is a far more respectable and sensitive diagnosis while still ensuring that trans folks have access to medical care (Buist & Stone 2014). However, there are still problems associated with diagnosis while in prison as one clinician refused to diagnose an inmate with GD because the incarcerated individual was attracted to women and liked cars (Hanssens et al. 2014).

Medical care for trans inmates will continue to be a major issue; however, there have been modest victories for incarcerated transgender men and women in the United States within recent years. For instance, in 2011, Wisconsin's antitrans law, the Inmate Sex Change Prevention Act, was found to be unconstitutional in *Fields v. Smith* on the grounds that preventing transgender prisoners from accessing transition-related care violated the Eighth Amendment's prohibition against cruel and unusual punishment (Glezer, McNeil & Binder 2013). Also in 2011, *Adams v. Bureau of Prisons* reversed the federal "freeze frame" policy that had prevented transgender prisoners from beginning transition-related care unless they could prove that they had already started it prior to incarceration (Glezer et al. 2013). Indeed, *Adams v. BOP* is an important victory for trans inmates as it prompted a major policy reversal for federal prisons, forcing government to begin guaranteeing access to hormone therapy and other care deemed medically necessary by doctors. Transgender BOP prisoners must now have access to "individualized assessment and evaluation." Also, "current, accepted standards of care will be used as a reference for developing the treatment plan," as outlined in the *Standards of Care* published by the World Professional Association for Transgender Health (WPATH). Finally, "treatment options will not be precluded solely due to level of services received, or lack of services, prior to incarceration." This tosses out the BOP's former "freeze frame" policy, whereby officials could refuse transition-related care for prisoners who could not prove they had started such treatment before being incarcerated. Such arbitrary, blanket bans of health care have been repeatedly found to be unconstitutional (Colopy 2012; Glezer et al. 2013).

One of the most noteworthy victories in recent years was the 2012 ruling that Massachusetts inmate Michelle (birth name: Robert) Kosilek would receive sex reassignment surgery because the "state's failure to provide it . . . violate[d] the Eighth Amendment protection against cruel and unusual punishment" (Ellement & Anderson 2014). However, this was a short-lived victory. As of December 2014, the court's ruling had been overturned and now Kosilek will not be granted sex reassignment surgery. Although correctional authorities have conceded to the legitimacy of Kosilek's gender identity, providing her with medical care, women's clothing, facial hair removal, hormones, and other personal property, the higher court found that this was adequate. Judge Thompson's dissent attacked the antiquated and often inaccurate ways in which society views sex and gender, stating that "the precedent the majority creates is damaging . . . it . . . aggrieves an already marginalized community, and enables correctional systems to further postpone their adjustment to the crumbling gender binary" (as cited in Ellement & Anderson 2014).

Judge Thompson's comments speak volumes to the problems associated with how detrimental to trans inmates this decision may be. Yes, it does matter that prison officials recognized Kosilek's gender identity and have acted in ways that respect and reaffirm that identity, but not to the extent by which it should. To force a woman to live out the rest of her life (Kosilek is serving a life sentence for the murder of her wife) in an all-male institution is the definition of deliberate indifference to the harm that has been done to Kosilek and the potential harm that may further be inflicted. This is something that must be considered for all transgender prisoners who wish to complete sex reassignment surgery.

Rape and sexual assault in prison

Prisoners in the United States and abroad face additional punishment and pains of imprisonment in addition to their original sentencing – one such abuse that those incarcerated experience is sexual violence. Just Detention International (JDI) reports that approximately 200,000 prisoners (including children) have been the victims of sexual abuse in US prisons, with half of the assaults occurring at the hands of prison staff (Beck & Johnson 2012; Beck, Berzofsky, & Krebs 2013; JDI 2015). While being raped in prison is often the punch-line to pop culture's sick joke, this is a very real problem, so much so that PREA was enacted specifically to "provide for the analysis of the incidence and effects of prison rape in Federal, State, and local institutions and to provide information, resources, recommendations and funding to protect individuals from prison rape" (Prison Rape Elimination Act 2003). Passing PREA was a step in the right direction, but it can be argued that little if any change has occurred since 2003. For example, the Bureau of Justice Statistics report on sexual victimization in prisons, as reported by correctional authorities, indicated that there were 589 "substantiated incidents of sexual violence in 2008, up 28 percent from 459 substantiated incidents reported in 2005" (Guerino & Beck 2011: n.p.). Whether rates of rape are increasing or reporting is improving remains to be seen. What is known is that the assaults that do occur, reported or not, have devastating consequences.

> The degrading experience caused damage to my self-esteem for many years ... I definitely felt that I did not own my own body. It was enough to convince me that my life did not belong to me and I was robbed of every single drop of dignity of a human being.
>
> *Cecilia Chung, transgender inmate, San Francisco County Jail*
> *Just Detention International 2005*

Incarcerated Queer identified persons experience sexual violence in prison at devastatingly higher rates, up to ten times higher, than heterosexual inmates (Beck et al. 2013; JDI 2015). Additionally, according to Colopy (2012), in California prisons, nearly 60 percent of trans inmates reported being sexually assaulted as opposed to only 4 percent of the general population. The rape problem in the US correctional system is pervasive and impacts men, women, and juveniles who are incarcerated. As CeCe McDonald, a formerly incarcerated trans woman, remarked: "Prisons aren't safe for anyone, and that's the key issue" (as cited in Hanssens et al. 2014).

Comparatively speaking, we remind you of the victimization faced in places like Cameroon as mentioned at the onset of this chapter. We also would like to draw special attention to the treatment of Queer-identified immigrants who are often seeking asylum from countries where they face violence based on their sexual and/or gender identity. Tabak and Levitan (2014) highlight the harms that are done to migrants who are being detained and indicate that this vulnerable population of LGBTI detainees oftentimes faces increased challenges and violence. Much like PREA, the European Court of Human Rights (ECHR) has found that forced segregation for protection should also be considered a violation of human rights. As evidenced, incarcerated Queer people experience pains of punishment well beyond their sentences. We must remember that correctional practices, while a means of social control, can have, at times, unintended and collateral consequences that further punish those who are especially vulnerable while incarcerated.

Recommended viewing

Cruel and Unusual, 2006 [Film] Directed by Janet Baus, Dan Hunt & Reid Williams. USA: Reid Productions.

References

Adams v. Bureau of Prisons. 716 F. Supp. 2d 107 (2010).

American Bar Association. 2010. *Standards on treatment of prisoners.* Accessed from http://www.americanbar.org/publications/criminal_justice_section_archive/crimjust_standards_treatmentprisoners.html#23–2.2.

American Civil Liberties Union. 2012. *Know your rights: Medical, dental and mental health care.* ACLU National Prison Project. Accessed from https://www.aclu.org/files/assets/know_your_rights_—_medical_mental_health_and_dental_july_2012.pdf.

Beck, A.J., Berzofsky, M., & Krebs, C. 2013. *Sexual victimization in prisons and jails reported by inmates, 2011–2012.* Washington, DC: Bureau of Justice Statistics.

Beck, A.J. & Johnson, C. 2012. *Sexual victimization reported by former inmates, 2008.* Washington, DC: Bureau of Justice Statistics.

Bell, B. 2014. *Six questions for transgender rights advocate Mara Keisling. ABC News,* August 16. Accessed from http://abcnews.go.com/blogs/politics/2014/08/6-questions-for-transgender-rights-advocate-mara-keisling/.

Brown, G.R. 2009. *Recommended revisions to the World Professional Association for Transgender Health's Standards of Care Section on Medical Care for Incarcerated Persons with Gender Identity Disorder. International Journal of Transgenderism,* 11, (2): 133–139.

Browne, A., Hastings, A., Kall, K., & diZerega, M. 2015. *Keeping vulnerable populations safe under PREA: Alternative strategies to the use of segregation in prisons and jails.* NY: Vera Institute of Justice.

Buist, C.L. & Stone, C. 2014. *Transgender victims and offenders: Failures of the United States criminal justice system and the necessity of queer criminology. Critical Criminology, 22,* (1): 35–47.

Canadian Press. 2013. *Gay former Ottawa jail guard gets $98K in homophobia suit: Robert Ranger endured "profoundly humiliating" homophobic harassment. Canadian Press.* July 26. Accessed from http://www.cbc.ca/news/canada/ottawa/gay-former-ottawa-jail-guard-gets-98k-in-homophobia-suit-1.1321771.

Carson, A.E. 2014. *Prisoners in 2013.* U.S. Department of Justice. Washington, DC: Bureau of Justice Statistics.

Coker v. Georgia. 433 U.S. 584 (1977).

Collins, W.C. 2004. *Supermax prisons and the constitution: Liability concerns in the extended control unit.* Washington, DC: National Institute of Corrections.

Colopy, T.W. 2012. *Setting gender identity free: Expanding treatment for transsexual inmates. Health Matrix: Journal of Law Medicine, 22:* 262–271.

Dolovich, S. 2009. *Cruelty, prison conditions, and the eighth amendment. New York University Law Review, 84*, (4): 881–972.

Editorial Board. 2015. *Men's central jail should be demolished. But what should replace it? Los Angeles Times*, January 4. Accessed from http://touch.latimes.com/#section/-1/article/p2p-82443952/.

Ellement, J.R. & Anderson, T. 2014. *Court denies inmate's sex-change surgery. Reverses ruling in 2012 Kosilek case; Sex-change surgery funding is at issue. The Boston Globe*, December 16. Accessed from http://www.bostonglobe.com/metro/2014/12/16/federal-appeals-court-overturns-ruling-ordering-sex-change-surgery-for-mass-prison-inmate/WqBuLuGI14yZ6nVoFCIfjK/story.html.

Farmer v. Brennan. 511. U.S. 825 (1984).

Fields v. Smith. 653 F. 3d. 550 (2011).

Furman v. Georgia. 408 U.S. 238 (1972).

Glaze, L.E. & Kaeble, D. 2014. *Correctional populations in the United States, 2013.* U.S. Department of Justice. Washington, DC: Bureau of Justice Statistics.

Glezer, A., McNeil, D.E., & Binder, R.L. 2013. *Transgendered and incarcerated: A review of the literature, current policies and laws, and ethics. Journal of American Academy Psychiatry Law, 41*: 551–559.

Grassian, S. 1983. *Psychopathological effects of solitary confinement. American Journal of Psychiatry, 140*, (11): 1450–1454.

Gregg v. Georgia. 438 U.S. 153 (1976).

Guerino, P. & Beck, A.J. 2011. *Sexual victimization reported by adult correctional authorities, 2007–2008.* Washington, DC: Bureau of Justice Statistics.

Hanson, A. 2011. Solitary confinement: Rumor or reality? Solitary confinement: Does it provoke mental illness? *Psychology Today*, August 25. Accessed from https://www.psychologytoday.com/blog/shrink-rap-today/201108/solitary-confinement-rumor-and-reality.

Hanssens, C., Moodie-Mills, A., Ritchie, A.J., Spade, D., & Vaid, U. 2014. *A roadmap for change: Federal policy recommendations for addressing the criminalization of LGBT people and people living with HIV*. New York, NY: Center for Gender & Sexuality Law at Columbia Law School.

Hauwert, M.C. 2015. *Op-ed: Transitioning as a guard at San Quentin State Prison. The Advocate*, March 3. Accessed from http://www.advocate.com/commentary/2015/03/03/op-ed-transitioning-guard-san-quentin-state-prison.

Holsinger, K. & Hodge, J.P. 2014. *The experiences of lesbian, gay, bisexual, and transgender girls in juvenile justice systems. Feminist Criminology*: 1–25.

Human Rights Watch. 2013. *Guilty by association: Human rights violations in the enforcements of Cameroon's anti-homosexuality law*. United States of America: Human Rights Watch.

Just Detention International. 2005. National prison rape elimination commission testimony of Cecilia Chung. Accessed from http://www.justdetention.org/en/NPREC/ceciliachung.aspx.

Just Detention International. 2015. The basics about abuse in U.S. detention. Accessed from http://www.justdetention.org/en/fact_sheets.aspx.

Kennedy v. Louisiana. 554 U.S. 407 (2008).

Klein, E. & Soltas, E. 2013. *Wonkbook: 11 facts about America's prison population. Washington Post.* Accessed from http://www.washingtonpost.com/blogs/wonkblog/wp/2013/08/13/wonkbook-11-facts-about-americas-prison-population.

Lenning, E. & Buist, C.L. 2012. *Social, psychological and economic challenges faced by transgender individuals and their significant others: Gaining insight through personal narratives. Culture, Health & Sexuality: An International Journal for Research, Intervention and Care, 15,* (1): 44–57.

Mack, S.K. 2013. *Gay former prison guard files discrimination lawsuit against state. Bangor Daily News,* May 7. Accessed from http://bangordailynews.com/2013/05/07/news/down-east/gay-former-prison-guard-files-discrimination-lawsuit-against-state/.

Majd, K., Marksamer, J., & Reyes, C. 2009. *Hidden injustice: Lesbian, gay, bisexual, and transgender youth in juvenile courts.* Washington, DC: Legal Services of Children, National Juvenile Defender Center and National Center for Lesbian Rights.

Margolin, E. 2014. *Does the LGBT movement ignore inmates? MSNBC,* November 14. Accessed from http://www.msnbc.com/msnbc/lgbt-prisoners-abuse.

Moodie-Mills, A. & Gilbert, C. 2014. *Restoring justice: A blueprint for ensuring fairness, safety, and supportive treatment of LGBT youth in the juvenile justice system.* Center for American Progress.

O'Keefe, M.L., Klebe, K., Stucker, A., Sturm, K., & Leggett, W. 2011. *One year longitudinal study of the psychological effects of administrative segregation.* United States Department of Justice. National Criminal Justice Statistics Service.

Perkinson, R. 1994. *Shackled justice: Florence federal penitentiary and the new politics of punishment. Social Justice, 21,* (3): 117–132.

Prison Rape Elimination Act of 2003. PREA Public Law 108–79. Accessed from http://www.gpo.gov/fdsys/pkg/PLAW-108publ79/pdf/PLAW-108publ79.pdf.

R. G. v. Koller. 415F. Supp. 2d 1129 (2006).

Shelley, Christopher A. 2009. *Transpeople and social justice. The Journal of Individual Psychology, 65,* (4): 386–396.

Tabak, S. & Levitan, R. 2014. *LGBTI migrants in immigration detention: A global perspective. Harvard Journal of Law & Gender, 37:* 1–42

Trop v. Dulles. 356 U.S. 86 (1958).

Ucar, A. 2014. *In the gay wing of L.A. men's Central Jail, it's not shanks and muggings but sewn gowns and tears. L.A. Weekly,* November 14. Accessed from http://www.laweekly.com/news/in-the-gay-wing-of-la-mens-central-jail-its-not-shanks-and-muggings-but-hand-sewn-gowns-and-tears-5218552.

6

FUTURE DIRECTIONS IN QUEER CRIMINOLOGY

The continued development of a sustainable queer criminology is paramount to examining and understanding the use of the criminal legal system as a means to control groups of people and individuals who identify outside of the gender binary and heteronormative landscape. Throughout this text, we have provided an array of examples from the United States and abroad that highlight the ways in which laws and attitudes surrounding sexuality and gender are used as weapons of the state to control the behavior of those who do not fit the societal norm. These examples demonstrate both the research that has already been done and illuminates areas in which the research is lacking, thus providing a roadmap for the future of queer criminology. In this chapter, we will revisit the areas of criminalizing queerness, law enforcement, legal systems, and corrections by focusing on the gaps within the bodies of literature in those areas. Then, we will consider how other (non-queer) criminologies can be strengthened by the consideration of Queer communities, and discuss why queer criminology must be intersectional, interdisciplinary, public, and in constant evolution.

Gaps in the literature

Perhaps the most significant challenge to developing a clear picture of Queer experiences with and within the criminal legal system is the relative lack of accurate data available (Finneran & Stephenson 2012; Gruenewald 2012). While it is true, as we hope to have demonstrated with this book, that there is a sizeable amount of qualitative and anecdotal evidence to highlight incidents of queer (in)justice around the world, quantitative data describing even the most common criminal justice interactions (e.g., queer arrest data) is largely nonexistent. While it is true that quantitative data has its own limitations, it would help to determine the magnitude of the problems exposed in the qualitative data. True, even if officers reported the sexual or gender identities of their arrestees as they do, for example, race, the picture would not be completely accurate (as officers may misidentify or citizens may not be truthful), but it would be an improvement on our current understanding. This is not to say that no quantitative data exists at all, and we have tried to highlight what is available as appropriate in the previous chapters, but that it is extremely limited in scope.

Chapter 2 focused on how queerness is criminalized throughout the world. As mentioned in Chapter 1, current religious freedom acts are being passed in the United States, and while they do not specifically criminalize sexual orientation and/or gender identity, they essentially allow for others to discriminate against the Queer community based on religious beliefs. While discrimination guised within freedom is not a new occurrence, we have to remind ourselves that we are well into the new millennium and still fighting for equity. The fight for equal treatment under the law is not something of the past – there are still issues that Queer people face on an everyday basis. Certainly, trans folks face stress, anxiety, and fear that cisgender people would rarely if ever have to encounter, let alone even think about. For instance, as of March 2015, there were several states in the United States considering legislation that would not only ban trans folks from using the bathroom of their choice, but that would criminalize the behavior up to a felony, with fines and possibly jail time as a result (Brodey & Lurie 2015). One such bill recently passed in Kentucky prevents trans students from using the bathroom of their choosing and instead forcing students to use the bathroom that corresponds to their biological sex. Trans students may use bathrooms designated for faculty use, or other accommodations, but only if the student makes a special request. Further, this does not address the prohibition of locker room or shower use, as it would be assumed that students would also have to use the locker room and shower that corresponds with their biological sex, and there is no information on whether or not special accommodations would be made for use of those facilities. These bills, much like the Indiana Religious Freedom Act, are almost always sponsored by conservative "family" organizations and backed by the Republican Party, and should serve as a reminder of the ways in which queerness is criminalized and bodies are controlled by the state. Conversely, California passed a bill into law that allows transgender students to use the facilities that match their gender identity and Democratic Senator Ricardo Lara noted that while some argue that allowing trans folks to use the facilities matching their gender identity can be problematic, some going so far as to imply that transgender men and women are sexual predators, he points out that there has not been any evidence, in fact not even a single report, of misconduct (Hansen & Maza 2013).

In addition to the trans population impacted by bathroom legislation, lesbians who self-identify as "butch," masculine, or gender-queer have addressed being bullied in the bathroom based on others' assumption about their sex and gender identity. Writing for the popular online site for lesbians, Autostraddle, which heralds itself as "news, entertainment, opinion, community and girl-on-girl culture," one editorial contributor tells of her personal experiences in public restrooms as other women fear her because they assume that her masculine presentation means that she is a man who has wandered into the ladies room, no doubt to assault them in some way.

> Since my gender presentation is most often mistaken for a teenage boy, the thought of using public bathrooms is anxiety-creating . . . I hate the second looks, the stares. . . . At the same time, I feel guilty and ashamed that my presence in the women's bathroom was read by this woman as a threat . . .

These are real fears, and while not always deemed as criminal or law-breaking behavior, the way in which Queer folks are made to feel is often controlling and unmanageable for some who merely want to use the restroom. Imagine how you would feel if you were so frightened that you may be arrested or, at the very least, accosted either physically or verbally because you used the restroom in a public place – how paralyzing that fear could be – so much so that it may keep you from engaging in the world around you, avoiding certain locations for fear that you might be confronted for using a facility that we all use on a daily basis. Perhaps that fear would keep you from these places, keep you in your home, out of the public purview. What these heteronormative gazes do is rob Queer people from obtaining and gaining human agency and social capital, which, criminological research has revealed, is a pathway to deviance and crime.

As we are well aware, legislation is changing every day, and therefore the experiences of individuals and groups are likely to change as well. However, issues regarding the criminalization of queerness quite possibly will always remain problematic. One of those reasons returns us to language and identity. New perspectives will develop, new ways of gender presentation will emerge, and, beyond that, we must remind ourselves that while this book has attempted to take the most inclusive stance we could, it can be troublesome to group all LGBTQ folks together. In Chapter 1, we discussed the influence of queer theoretical approaches that have focused on the deconstruction of categories. We further highlighted the work of Sedgwick (1990), who so accurately noted that an individual will identify herself or himself in a myriad of ways that may in fact not align with how the public would identify someone. We must always keep this in mind when we are examining the criminalization of queerness – reminding ourselves, fellow scholars, and agents in the criminal legal field that while identity can be fixed for some, for others it is dynamic and ever changing – this is also true of sexual orientation. The possibility of this fluidity makes categorization difficult at best, although, as we have argued, categories can be empowering as well. In many ways, we still live in a monochromatic world, outsiders looking in will continue to categorize others in efforts to understand the world in which they live, and until that stops, using categories and descriptions to empower and impede continues.

Of each of the three arms of the criminal legal system (i.e. law enforcement, legal systems, corrections), our understanding of Queer experiences with and as law enforcement officers is perhaps the most complete. Still, the research that does exist only scratches the surface. As Chapter 3 demonstrates, there is evidence that in their interactions with police officers, Queer people (especially trans people) face selective enforcement, harassment, and brutality at significantly greater rates than the general public (e.g. Buist & Stone 2014; Dwyer 2011; Greenberg 2011; NCAVP 2012). Queer criminology should seek to contextualize these experiences beyond what we already know. In particular, the victims of police brutality can vastly improve our understanding of how our multiple identities can increase or decrease our risk of victimization. Further, the focus of that research should not just be on the victims, but also on the officers that engage in abusing Queer citizens. Research in this area can then be used to develop and implement training protocols for law enforcement, especially in the area of policing diverse communities.

It is not enough to respond to reported incidents of disproportionate contact and heightened police victimization of Queer people by simply noting that within policing, just like any occupation, there are good and bad representatives of the law. This argument does not hold water in response to racist behavior conducted by law enforcement officers either. As we have indicated with our past discussion, we cannot continue to allow agents of social control, who have the most interaction with the public, to abuse their powers and use their authority to brutalize citizens – regardless of their guilt or innocence. We do not expect perfection but we do, as we should, expect our officers of the law to be held to a higher standard and, in turn, we should not continue to accept these abuses of power as a means to illegally control and victimize the people. In addition to these problems between law enforcement and civilians, it is imperative that we understand that men and women working within the existing paramilitaristic and hyper-masculine structure of policing are also victims of harassment, discrimination, and violence because of their sexual orientation and/or gender identity, and that the abuses they face are not unlike the abuses the public faces. We should not sit back, idly by, and assume that these are only private problems when they are in fact public issues that affect all of us (Mills 1959), and therefore should concern all of us regardless of sexual orientation or gender identity.

It is not enough to simply describe these incidents – a queer criminology must seek to use empirical data to influence policy and practice, and that cannot be done by confining our work to academic circles. Researchers must focus on systemic problems as well, such as examining the real possibility that the institutions within the criminal legal system, like patriarchal law enforcement agencies, are heteronormative and homophobic (Ball 2014) and therefore those systems must change in order for the civilians to reap any benefits from policy and practice. As noted in Chapter 3, there has been some success in places like England and Wales and Ontario, among others, that once departmental policy was changed and, importantly, deviations from the policy enforced, Queer citizens as well as Queer officers' feelings of safety and acceptance increased.

Chapter 4 revealed that a criminological understanding of Queer experiences within legal systems is perhaps where there is the most work to be done. It is true that quite a bit of research and debate exists in the areas of hate crimes and hate crime legislation (e.g. European Union Agency for Fundamental Rights 2014; Garland & Chakraborti 2012; Meyer 2014; NCAVP 2014; Sullaway 2004), but the truth is that hate crimes occur far less often than other crimes that Queer people are likely to fall victim to, thus resulting in an interaction with the legal system. For example, there must be more research centered on the courtroom experiences of Queer victims of domestic violence and sexual assault. The work that has been done on bias in the courtroom (e.g. Brower 2011; Cramer 2002; Meidinger 2012; Shay 2014; Shortnacy 2001) implies that Queer victims who seek legal protections from violence would face greater barriers than non-Queer victims, and should therefore be a focus of future research.

Even less is known about the disparate sentencing of Queer offenders, and the primary focus of research in this area has been on the rarest form of punishment – the death penalty (e.g., Farr 2000; Mogul 2005; Shortnacy 2001). We know little about whether or not Queer offenders committing more common, nonviolent crimes are sentenced with leniency or are sentenced more harshly than non-Queer offenders. Again, this is because data on sexual or gender identity is not collected in the same way that other demographic information is. An overwhelming amount of research demonstrates that race influences sentencing outcomes (see Mitchell 2005), which begs the question, what might we learn if we explore the intersection of race and actual or perceived sexual or gender identity as they relate to judicial decision making? More research on sentencing outcomes will not only tell us more about Queer experiences in the courtroom, but will reveal new avenues for research in the area of corrections, which is also in need of attention.

Further, the inequality that Queer people face in court systems throughout the world is unacceptable. Here in the United States, where we tout the importance of "justice for all," we have rarely seen this play out in a court of law with not only Queer folks but poor people of color as well. As research has indicated, Blacks are more likely to be sentenced, and for longer periods, than whites for comparable crimes. Further, Blacks are more likely to receive the sentence of death, especially if their victims are white, and the poor are the least likely group to have capable representation. We know, as highlighted in Chapter 4, that Queer people as adult and juveniles have received harsher sentences in some cases, but the empirical data is still inadequate and thus in need of attention.

As pointed out in Chapter 5, there is a dearth of research in the area of community corrections. Most of what we know about Queer encounters with corrections centers around the incarceration of Queer people. While there is a mass incarceration epidemic that should not be ignored, especially in the United States, offenders more often face punishments of probation and those who are incarcerated are likely to experience some sort of postincarceration surveillance. Thus, it is necessary to understand the conditions that Queer offenders face under these types of correctional supervision. As is the case with law enforcement and legal systems, it is safe to assume that Queer offenders face unique challenges, and an understanding of those challenges would enhance what we already know about probationers, parolees, and barriers to reentry. For example, how much harder is it for a Queer parolee to gain employment than other parolees? What about Queer parolees of color? Knowing how queerness and intersectionality affects one's correctional experiences can lead us towards the development of more effective sanctions and reentry services.

Further, as Chapter 5 indicated, the majority of the research on corrections and the Queer community has been couched within the needs and the experiences of transgender offenders and inmates. Certainly, we do not disagree that this should be a major focus of the research, as we have indicated that Queer-identified inmates, but especially trans identified inmates, face an increased likelihood of victimization. Therefore, exploring the experiences of Queer, but perhaps especially trans, offenders once they have been released from incarceration is wholly important to queer criminology. For instance, research from the National Transgender Discrimination Survey found that 26 percent of trans folks lost their jobs based on their gender identity, while 50 percent had experienced on-the-job harassment based on their gender identity. If we focus on the percentage of trans individuals who lost their job solely because of their identity, think about the heightened impact that having a criminal record would have on trans people. Research has found that most employers would not hire the formerly incarcerated (Raphael 2008), contributing to the millions of parolees who are without legitimate work. The "ban the box" initiative is working to help increase work opportunities for job seekers with criminal records, but this does not speak to the problems associated with being transgender *and* an ex-con.

As mentioned, the literature that exists on the incarceration of Queer people appears to be the only area of LGBTQ-focused research where the transgender community is concentrated on to a greater degree than the lesbian and gay community. While past research ignored transgender inmates and instead focused exclusively on consensual and unwanted same-sex sexual encounters, they have emerged to be a central focus. Certainly, as trans people become more visible and as the rights of transgender inmates continue to be defined by the courts, new avenues of research will be exposed. This should not, however, undermine the importance of considering the correctional experiences of all Queer people. Bisexuals, for example, are virtually invisible in all areas of criminological research.

In large part due to the media, the general public often thinks about the criminal legal system in terms of the most sensational issues, such as police brutality and the death penalty, and any public debate around these issues is almost always predicated by extraordinary and (usually) rare, high-profile criminal cases. Being less interesting, issues like police training, the terms of probation, or the classification of inmates rarely get attention. As we can see from the research high-lighted in this book, criminologists focusing on Queer issues also tend to gravitate towards the sensational. While the research on topics like police violence, hate crimes, and the death penalty is important and should continue, there must also be a shift in focus towards the more mundane – the everyday issues of the criminal legal system that affect greater numbers of people, such as those mentioned above.

Queer(ing) criminology

Queer criminology is more than simply adding sexuality or gender identity as a variable to research. Indeed, as described in Chapter 1, queer criminology is a criminology that investigates, criticizes and challenges heteronormative systems of oppression in the context of the criminal legal system. This is not to say, however, that other (non-Queer) criminologies cannot benefit from the consideration of sexualized and gendered experiences in the same way that they consider how an individual's experiences in the criminal legal system are connected to sex, race, age, and class. While we are not advocating an "add Queer and stir" approach to criminological research, it is necessary to begin adding sexual and gender identities as inde-pendent variables alongside sex, race, age, socioeconomic status, and other demographic characteristics. By failing to recognize sexuality and gender identity as integral to one's experiences in the same man-ner in which we recognize the significance of race or social class, we reinforce the stereotype that being Queer is a deviant act as opposed to an inherent part of one's self and something that has bearing on experiences and outcomes in the criminal legal system. There must be a conscious effort to remove the "sexuality or gender as deviant" stigma that criminologists have historically been a part of perpetuat-ing (Woods 2014, 2015).

Since its birth in the 1870s, modern criminology has focused on sexual orientation and gender identity in some form or fash-ion (Woods 2015). The manner and degree to which they have been considered, however, has fluctuated in concert with historical developments and shifts in criminological thought (Woods 2014, 2015). What was quite consistent however, until roughly the 1970s, is that sexual minorities and gender nonconforming individuals were framed by criminologists in the same way they were framed by the general public – as (criminal) deviants. Woods (2014) points out that even critical criminology, which is literally built on the premise that constructions of crime and criminality should be challenged, has been guilty of promoting the "homosexuality as deviant" stereotype. Even as social reaction and labeling theories gained popularity, homosexuality in and of itself was framed by criminologists like Lemert and Becker as an inherently deviant behavior and, although they "did not necessarily intend to stigmatize LGBTQ people, their inability to engage in critical discourse outside the sexual deviancy framework illustrates that their early critical perspectives rely on *outdated* ways of thinking about sexuality and gender identity that are damaging to LGBTQ people today" (Woods 2014: 10, emphasis added). Their perspectives, though dated now, were arguably within the norm at the time and reflected the historical moment in which they existed. The more Queer-affirming criminological research that we are seeing today has emerged on the heels of and likely as a result of great social and political advances for Queer people more generally (Panfil 2013). Thus, the historical moment matters in terms of how Queer people will be framed and included within criminological research.

Despite positive advances, criminological work still reflects stereotypes about Queer people and typical (i.e., white, middle class, male) social constructions of queerness. Panfil (2013) argues that this may be why the literature on Queer victimization is relatively saturated and conversely why there is little research on Queer offending beyond that which is focused on sex crimes like prostitution. She notes that "[b]eing regarded as passive, effeminate, middle-class, and white essentially removes gay men from consideration as violent offenders" (Panfil 2013: 103). In short, criminologists construct our hypotheses and design our research around our preconceived notions about people.

The practice of constructing research around preconceived notions and limited categories reveals another dilemma with the "add Queer and stir" approach. As discussed in depth in Chapter 1, the LGBT acronym is no longer sufficient to capture all of the identities that may fall under the umbrella of Queer. Lesbian, gay, bisexual, and transgender are simply starting points for classifying sexual and gender identities, so even research that includes them as independent variables will be limited. Not only do Queer people use a much more expansive dictionary to describe their identities (see Lenning 2009), but the language that they use may change rapidly, thus making research instruments tricky to design and replicate over time. Moreover, identity in and of itself may not capture what we are truly attempting to measure. If we want to know more about the violence faced by transgender individuals, for example, we need to capture both gender orientation and gender presentation, as one may be more explanatory than the other (Lenning 2009).

The complicated nature of measuring and understanding the impact of sexuality and gender on crime and justice issues may be exactly why criminology has largely avoided doing so. It is also quite possible that sexuality and gender are ignored for fear of being politically incorrect. As Panfil (2013) argues, some criminologists may hesitate to recognize and investigate Queer people, especially as violent offenders, in fear of further marginalizing them. Regardless of why Queer experiences in general (and Queer offending more specifically) have not historically been a focus of criminological inquiry, it is clear that both deserve greater attention, and the responsibility of doing that should not lie only within the realm of queer criminology.

Sustaining and growing queer criminology

Relative to criminology more generally and critical criminology more specifically, queer criminology is in its infancy. Indeed, it is only in the last few years that queer criminology has begun to establish a presence among academic circles, been given undivided attention by scholarly journals (e.g. a special issue of *Critical Criminology: An International Journal*), been the sole focus of scholarly books (e.g. Mogul, Ritchie, & Whitlock 2011; Peterson & Panfil 2014), and been recognized at the meetings of major organizations like the American Society of Criminology. This means that we are in a critical moment in the history of the field, and that today's pioneers of queer criminology play a crucial role in defining and shaping its future. What this book has revealed is that queer criminology must follow a path of intersectional, interdisciplinary, and public scholarship that is designed to adapt to the changing landscape of the Queer experience.

> There is no such thing as a single-issue struggle because we do not live single-issue lives.
>
> *Audre Lorde 2007, p. 138*

If queer criminology is "queer" because of its focus on deconstructing and challenging the role that the criminal legal system plays in the oppression of Queer people, then it must be committed to recognizing and exploring intersectionality. "Given that racism, sexism, and social class inequality make possible many forms of anti-queer violence," both interpersonal and institutional, "challenges to these forms of abuse must not merely consider homophobia but also account for other dimensions of inequality" (Meyer 2014: 116). For example, Black, poor, transgender women are not disproportionately targets of violence just because of homophobia or transphobia. Their victimization can only be understood by examining a web of racism, classism, sexism, and homophobia (Meyer 2012). To ignore this web is reductionist, and dilutes queer criminology in the same way that essentialism diluted feminist criminology with the assumption "that all women are oppressed by all men in exactly the same ways or that there is one unified experience of dominance experienced by women" (Burgess-Proctor 2006: 34). All Queer people are not, in fact, created equal, and a common identity of Queer does not make Queer experiences homogeneous. This returns us to the ongoing debate in this book, primarily as indicated here and in Chapter 1, about these ideas surrounding deconstruction as well as the impact of categorical description. We cannot stress enough that we see the validity in both approaches and we are not willing to choose one over the other, because our goal here has been to strive for inclusion in order to expand the scope of the research.

Further, "employing an intersectional approach to examine the lives of LGBT people necessitates not only including queer people who are oppressed along multiple axes of inequality, but also moving beyond frameworks that construct homophobia as the most predominant form of oppression confronting LGBT people" (Meyer 2012: 869). This is especially true as Queer people continue to win their fight for civil rights. Just as *Brown v. Board of Education* did not halt institutionalized racism, neither will *Lawrence v. Texas* end institutionalized homophobia and heterosexism. The battle for Queer civil rights (e.g. marriage) has in large part been fought by the most privileged (white, middle-class, male) Queer people, and those are the individuals that will most immediately reap the benefits. Low-income, Queer people of color will continue to face discrimination in large part due to their race and class, not their sexuality or gender identity. Thus, there must be a continued focus on how the matrix of domination plays out within the criminal legal system.

That said, it should also be noted that the make-up of the academy must more closely reflect the population we are studying. At present, the majority of criminological research that might be considered "queer" is being conducted by people who arguably fit the description of the most privileged (i.e. white, middle-class, and residing in the global North) – including the authors of this book. In truth, these privileges describe most scholars of popular and contemporary criminology, so "diversifying" the field is far easier said than done. Given, however, that the focus of queer criminology is to challenge systems of oppression, there must be a focus on elevating the voices that reflect those most oppressed.

In addition to recognizing and representing all of the possible dimensions of identity, research in queer criminology must also embrace an interdisciplinary approach. It behooves us to engage the scholarship that has been done in the realm of legal studies, psychology, and others in order to improve and not reinvent the wheel, so to speak. For example, imagine the possibility of combining the legal literature on courtroom bias (e.g. Brower 2011; Cramer 2002; Shay 2014) or police brutality (e.g. Buist & Stone 2014; Dwyer 2011; Greenberg 2011; NCAVP 2012) with the psychological study of implicit (i.e. unconscious) bias towards the Queer community. Only when we can understand and harness the myriad causes of discrimination can we subvert them, and that is a task far too great for one field.

In addition to blending disciplinary approaches, we must look outside of academia for information and knowledge. Much of what we know about Queer experiences with the criminal legal system does not come from research conducted by criminologists or, for that matter, even academics. By and large, it is journalists (most often working for LGBTQ publications), nongovernmental agencies, and other government-employed or independent groups of researchers that are uncovering and reporting them, such as those that are cited in this book. This is not necessarily a bad thing, as the academy has proven to have a rather limited audience, inasmuch as academic books are cost-prohibitive and peer-reviewed journals are not readily available to the general public as of yet and, even if they were, still wouldn't fit the definition of "accessible." Rather, this is a reminder that a transformative queer criminology must also be a public criminology, one that embraces and utilizes the power of technology and global interconnectivity, such as that found in new media.

TWEET: Roommate asked for the room till midnight. I went into molly's room and turned on my webcam. I saw him making out with a dude. Yay.

Dharun Ravi, September 19, 2010, three days before his
roommate jumped off of the George Washington Bridge
Foderaro 2010

New media is an accessible vehicle for gleaning information and an opportunity for queer criminology to both grow and affect social change. While traditional forms of media largely ignore or minimize crimes against the Queer community, new media has overwhelmingly exposed them. In the spirit of cultural criminology, queer criminologists must recognize and explore how "criminals and those criminalized construct their own meanings by their use of decentralized media" (Ferrell 2013: 261). If not for Facebook, Twitter, Tumblr, and Instagram, the tragic deaths of Brittany Stergis, Betty Skinner, Kandy Hall, Zoraida Reyes, and Mia Henderson, all transgender women murdered in 2014, may have gone unnoticed. Unlike traditional media, and certainly unlike academia, new media provided a forum for a much-needed conversation about the devaluing of trans lives, particularly for people of color.

Though the deaths of white Queer people more often make it to the mainstream media, it is still often on the heels of a social media firestorm. The suicide of 17-year-old Leelah Alcorn, a young, transgender teenager from Ohio, did make national headlines, but only after she posted her suicide note to the social media site Tumblr. In her note, Leelah wrote, "the only way I will rest in peace is if one day transgender people aren't treated the way I was, they're treated like humans, with valid feelings and human rights. . . . My death needs to mean something" (Corcoran & Spargo 2015). Tyler Clementi, a college freshman, likely would not have taken his own life by jumping off of the George Washington Bridge had his roommate not tweeted about and livestreamed video of him having an intimate encounter with another man in his dorm room. Thus, queer criminology would be incomplete if we did not take social media seriously as both a vehicle for victimization and offending, and as a tool for exploration, exposure, and transformation. New media must be recognized as an accessible forum for queer engagement and as central to making queer criminology a public criminology (Uggen & Inderbitzin 2010).

What new media reveals distinctly is that the inconsistent evolution of Queer rights is another complication to queer criminological research, inasmuch as Queer rights are changing (both for the better and the worse) on a daily basis. Indeed, by the time you are reading this book, it is entirely likely that some (if not many) of the laws that we highlight will have changed, so an ongoing challenge for queer criminologists is the constantly changing landscape of the Queer experience. Thus, queer criminology must be in constant evolution – in concert with and in reaction to the advancement of Queer rights (both within and outside of the criminal legal system) and the resulting backlash.

> Fix society. Please.
>
> *Leelah Alcorn, December 28, 2014, suicide*
> *note (Corcoran & Spargo 2015)*

The sheer magnitude of the Queer struggle broadly—and with the criminal legal system narrowly—is, in and of itself, a roadblock to timely change. As we hope to have demonstrated here, the struggle is complex, changing, and manifests differently based on a variety of factors, including individual identities and presentations, geography, culture, history, and political climate. Not only does this present a daunting task to queer criminologists, it creates a challenge to local, state, national and global criminal legal systems. While queer criminologists should focus their immediate attention on throwing "bricks through establishment or mainstream criminology's windows" in the spirit of critical criminology (DeKeseredy & Dragiewicz 2011: 2), citizens and criminal legal professionals alike must commit to a more egalitarian world and to the development of a criminal *justice* system, and to do so will mean tearing down the suffocating walls of (in)justice that have been built around us, one brick at a time.

References

Ball, M. 2014. *What's queer about queer criminology?* In Peterson, D. & Panfil, V. (eds.), *Handbook of LGBT communities, crime, and justice* (pp. 531–555). New York, NY: Springer.

Brodey, S. & Lurie, J. 2015. *Get ready for the conservative assault on where transgender Americans pee. Mother Jones*, March 9. Accessed from http://www.mother jones.com/politics/2015/03/transgender-bathroom-discrimination-bills.

Brower, T. 2011. *Twelve angry – and sometimes alienated – men: The experiences and treatment of lesbians and gay men during jury service. Drake Law Review,* 59: 669–706.

Buist, C.L. & Stone, C. 2014. *Transgender victims and offenders: Failures of the United States criminal justice system and the necessity of queer criminology. Critical Criminology, 22,* (1): 35–47.

Burgess-Proctor, A. 2006. *Intersections of race, class, gender, and crime: Future directions for feminist criminology. Feminist Criminology, 1*, (1): 27–47.

Corcoran, K. & Spargo, C. 2015. *Suicide note of 17-year-old transgender girl is DELETED from her Tumblr page after her Christian parents demand message blaming them for her death be removed. Daily Mail*, January 3. Accessed from http:// www.dailymail.co.uk/news/article-2895534/Heartbreaking-suicide-note-17-year-old-transgender-girl-DELETED-Tumblr-page-candlelit-vigils-held-honor.html.

Cramer, A. C. 2002. *Discovering and addressing sexual orientation bias in Arizona's legal system. Journal of Gender, Social Policy & the Law, 11*, (1): 25–37.

DeKeseredy, W. & Dragiewicz, M. (eds.) 2011. *Handbook of critical criminology*. New York, NY: Routledge.

Dwyer, A. 2011. *"It's not like we're going to jump them": How transgressing heteronormativity shapes police interactions with LGBT young people. Youth Justice, 11*, (3): 203–220.

European Union Agency for Fundamental Rights. 2014. *EU LGBT survey: European Union lesbian, gay, bisexual and transgender survey*. Luxembourg: Publications Office of the European Union.

Farr, Kathryn Ann. 2000. *Defeminizing and dehumanizing female murderers: Depictions of lesbians on death row. Women & Criminal Justice, 11*, (1): 49–66.

Ferrell, Jeff. 2013. *Cultural criminology and the politics of meaning. Critical Criminology, 21*, (3): 257–271.

Finneran, Catherine & Stephenson, Rob. 2012. *Intimate partner violence among men who have sex with men: A systematic review. Trauma, Violence, & Abuse, 14*, (2): 168–185.

Foderaro, L. 2010. *Private moment made public, then a fatal jump. New York Times*, September 29. Accessed from http://www.nytimes.com/2010/09/30/nyregion/30suicide.html?_r=0.

Garland, Jon & Chakraborti, Neil. 2012. *Divided by a common concept? Assessing the implications of different conceptualizations of hate crime in the European Union. European Journal of Criminology, 9*, (10): 38–51.

Greenberg, K. 2011. *Still hidden in the closet: Trans women and domestic violence. Berkeley Journal of Gender, Law & Justice*: 198–251.

Gruenewald, J. 2012. *Are anti-LGBT homicides in the United States unique? Journal of Interpersonal Violence, 27*, (18): 3601–3623.

Hansen, T. & Maza, C. 2013. *"The biggest con in the world": Fox News reacts to California student gender Identity Bill. Media Matters for America*, August 14. Accessed from http://mediamatters.org/research/2013/08/14/the-biggest-con-in-the-world-fox-news-reacts-to/195401.

Kate. 2013. *Butch please: Butch in the bathroom. Autostraddle*. May 3. Accessed from http://www.autostraddle.com/butch-please-butch-in-the-bathroom175366/.

Lenning, E. 2009. *Moving beyond the binary: Exploring the dimensions of gender presentation and orientation. International Journal of Social Inquiry, 2,* (2): 38–54.

Lorde, A. 2007. *Sister Outsider: Essays & Speeches.* Berkeley, CA: Crossing Press.

Meidinger, M.H. 2012. *Peeking under the covers: Taking a closer look at prosecutorial decision-making involving queer youth and statutory rape. Boston College Journal of Law & Social Justice, 32,* (2): 421–451.

Meyer, D. 2012. *An intersectional analysis of lesbian, gay, bisexual, and transgender (LGBT) people's evaluations of anti-queer violence. Gender & Society, 26,* (6): 849–873.

Meyer, D. 2014. *Resisting hate crime discourse: Queer and intersectional challenges to neoliberal hate crime laws. Critical Criminology, 22:* 113–125.

Mills, C.W. 1959. *The sociological imagination.* New York, NY: Oxford University Press.

Mitchell, O. 2005. *A meta-analysis of race and sentencing research: explaining the inconsistencies. Journal of Quantitative Criminology, 21,* (4): 439–466.

Mogul, J.L. 2005. *The dykier, the butcher, the better: The state's use of homophobia and sexism to execute women in the United States. New York City Law Review, 8:* 473–493.

Mogul, J.L., Ritchie, A., & Whitlock, K. 2011. *Queer (in)Justice: The criminalization of LGBT people in the United States.* Boston, MA: Beacon Press.

National Coalition of Anti-Violence Programs. 2012. *Lesbian, gay, bisexual, transgender, queer and HIV-affected hate violence in 2012.* New York, NY: National Coalition of Anti-Violence Programs.

National Coalition of Anti-Violence Programs. 2014. *Lesbian, gay, bisexual, transgender, queer, and HIV-affected hate violence in 2013.* New York, NY: National Coalition of Anti-Violence Programs.

Panfil, V. 2013. *Better left unsaid? The role of agency in queer criminological research. Critical Criminology, 22,* (1): 99–111.

Peterson, D. & Panfil, V. (eds.) 2014. *Handbook of LGBT communities, crime, and justice.* New York, NY: Springer.

Raphael, S. 2008. *The employment prospects of ex-offenders. Focus, 25,* (2): 21–26.

Sedgwick, E. 1990. *Epistemology of the closet.* Berkeley, CA: University of California Press.

Shay, G. 2014. *In the box: Voir dire on LGBT issues in changing times. Harvard Journal of Law & Gender, 37:* 407–457.

Shortnacy, M.B. 2001. *Guilty and gay, a recipe for execution in American courtrooms: Sexual orientation as a tool for prosecutorial misconduct in death penalty cases. American University Law Review, 51,* (2): 309–365.

Sullaway, M. 2004. *Psychological perspectives on hate crime laws. Psychology, Public Policy, and Law, 10,* (3): 250–292.

Uggen, C. & Inderbitzin, M. 2010. *Public criminologies. Criminology & Public Policy, 9,* (4): 725–749.

Woods, J.B. 2014. *Queer contestations and the future of a "critical" queer criminology. Critical Criminology, 22,* (1): 5–19.

Woods, J.B. 2015. *The birth of modern criminology and gendered constructions of homosexual criminal identity. Journal of Homosexuality, 62:* 131–166.

Wynn, M. 2015. *Transgender bathroom bill passes KY Senate. The Courier-Journal,* March 1. Accessed from http://www.courier-journal.com/story/news/politics/ky-legislature/2015/02/27/transgender-bathroom-bill-passes-kentucky-senate/24130083/.

POSTSCRIPT

After this book went into production, on June 26, 2015, the Supreme Court of the United States in a landmark decision ruled (5–4) in favor of marriage equality in all 50 states recognizing the constitutional right to marry. Several same-sex marriage cases were consolidated under *Obergefell v. Hodges*; *Bourke v. Beshear*, *DeBoer v. Snyder*, and *Tanco v. Haslam*. In the decision, written by Justice Kennedy, the Court states that the Fourteenth Amendment's Due Process and Equal Protection clauses have been invoked in the past, citing several cases – one of which is the well-known *Loving v. Virginia* in which the court found that laws prohibiting interracial marriage were unconstitutional. Kennedy (2015: 4) writes, "same-sex couples are denied benefits afforded opposite-sex couples . . . this denial works a grave and continuing harm, serving to disrespect and subordinate gays and lesbians."

As we write this, we celebrate, knowing that this is truly a historic day in US history, but we should remain aware of the myriad ways in which Queer folks are still discriminated against within the criminal legal system and although we should recognize the magnitude of these events, we must remain vigilant in our fight against prejudice and discrimination. We anticipate interpersonal discrimination via religious freedom bills much like the recent bill passed in Indiana that we discussed in detail earlier in the book. With that being noted, we continue to recognize the impact of this historical decision and we echo Justice Kennedy's (2015: 33 emphasis in original) final thoughts, "they ask for equal dignity in the eyes of the law. The Constitution grants them that right . . . *It is so ordered.*"

Reference

Kennedy, A. 2015. *Obergefell v. Hodges.* 576 U.S. ___.

INDEX

CPSIA information can be obtained
at www.ICGtesting.com
Printed in the USA
FSHW020149061218
54261FS

9 781138 824379